CW01310219

# THE STRUGGLES OF UNLOVED WOMEN

*A Story Behind Every Door*

## LINDA K. COLBERT

WESTBOW
PRESS®
A DIVISION OF THOMAS NELSON
& ZONDERVAN

Copyright © 2016 Linda Colbert.

All rights reserved. No part of this book may be used or reproduced by any means, graphic, electronic, or mechanical, including photocopying, recording, taping or by any information storage retrieval system without the written permission of the author except in the case of brief quotations embodied in critical articles and reviews.

Scripture taken from the Holy Bible, NEW INTERNATIONAL VERSION®. Copyright © 1973, 1978, 1984, 2011 by Biblica, Inc. All rights reserved worldwide. Used by permission. NEW INTERNATIONAL VERSION® and NIV® are registered trademarks of Biblica, Inc. Use of either trademark for the offering of goods or services requires the prior written consent of Biblica US, Inc.

All Scripture quotations in this publications are from The Message. Copyright © by Eugene H. Peterson 1993, 1994, 1995, 1996, 2000, 2001, 2002. Used by permission of NavPress Publishing Group.

New Revised Standard Version Bible, copyright © 1989, Division of Christian Education of the National Council of the Churches of Christ in the United States of America. Used by permission. All rights reserved.

WestBow Press books may be ordered through booksellers or by contacting:

WestBow Press
A Division of Thomas Nelson & Zondervan
1663 Liberty Drive
Bloomington, IN 47403
www.westbowpress.com
1 (866) 928-1240

Because of the dynamic nature of the Internet, any web addresses or links contained in this book may have changed since publication and may no longer be valid. The views expressed in this work are solely those of the author and do not necessarily reflect the views of the publisher, and the publisher hereby disclaims any responsibility for them.

Any people depicted in stock imagery provided by Thinkstock are models, and such images are being used for illustrative purposes only. Certain stock imagery © Thinkstock.

ISBN: 978-1-5127-5499-5 (sc)
ISBN: 978-1-5127-5500-8 (hc)
ISBN: 978-1-5127-5498-8 (e)

Library of Congress Control Number: 2016914157

Print information available on the last page.

WestBow Press rev. date: 10/14/2016

# Contents

Dedication ................................................................... vii

Acknowledgements ........................................................ ix

Foreword ................................................................... xiii

Introduction ................................................................ xv

1. Behind Door One .................................................... 1
   The Woman of Samaria: Discovering the Living Water

2. Behind Door Two ................................................... 17
   Abigail: When Beauty Marries a Fool

3. Behind Door Three ................................................. 33
   Mary Magdalene: From Demons to Devotion

4. Behind Door Four .................................................. 50
   Tamar: A Defiled Princess in Isolation

5. Behind Door Five ................................................... 67
   Hannah: A Prayer and a Vow Fulfilled

6. Behind Door Six ..................................................... 83
   Leah: Comforted by Her Children

7. Behind Door Seven ................................................ 102
   Esther: A Queen for Such a Time as This

8. Behind Door Eight .................................................................. 124
   Jezebel: The Wicked Shall Cease from Troubling

9. Behind Door Nine ....................................................................145
   Naomi: Surviving the Storms of Widowhood

10. Behind Door Ten ................................................................. 164
    Mary: The Sorrowful Mother at the Cross

    Notes ........................................................................................ 185

# Dedication

To,
My husband and dearest friend, Aubrey,
A man who loves God's people and a treasured gift to me.

For,
My beloved mother, Arlone Paschal and
my dear sister, Cynthia Marie,
God's grace is sufficient through every struggle.

In Loving Memory of,
Pastor Claybon Lea, Sr.
An extraordinary man and pastor who taught us so much.

# Acknowledgements

I cannot do anything apart from God! He *is* my Rock and the joy of my salvation! God provides all that I need to accomplish His desires for me. Therefore, I give Him all the glory, honor, and praise for His presence and guidance throughout this first book project. I thank God for the vision. *The Struggles of Unloved Women*, is nothing like I envisioned, but I believe that this book says everything that God intended for me to say.

I am so grateful for my husband, Aubrey Wilford Colbert, my companion for life. I thank God for your quiet presence throughout the writing of this book and for your generosity. Thank you for teaching me how to develop my gifts and for encouraging me to launch out into deeper waters. I am grateful for your strength, wisdom, discernment, prayers, and especially your constructive advice. You made sure that the doctrine is sound and that is invaluable.

I thank God for my dear sister and friend, Gwendolyn Colbert. God gave you amazing eyes to see what most people cannot see! I appreciate you for all the times you came into my room, sat with me as I read to you, and told me exactly what you could see! I love you my faithful companion. I am truly grateful for my siblings—much love to you all. God has been gracious to all of us. We will always be together.

*Acknowledgements*

I want to thank my two friends and editors, Carolyn Softly and Monica Netherly—two dynamic sisters in Christ! You are precious, strong women of God in whom I am deeply indebted. Thank you for your time and honesty and for making this a rewarding, learning experience. I am grateful for my dear friends and sisters in Christ, Dr. Dorothy Pettigrew and Reverend Constance "CJ" Jackson. I thank God for your unwavering friendship, godly examples, wisdom, and prayers. Our love for the Lord and each other will always be the glue that holds us together.

I have gained an even greater appreciation for time. Who would have thought that much of this book would be written at the beauty shop? To my friend Lorna Jackson, I am deeply grateful for the space—called my office—you provided for me at your salon. I love you for your kindness and generosity. I thank God for women like Carol Vinson Lea—the epitome of a First Lady. You are simply beautiful, inside and outside. Thank you for teaching us how to serve and for modeling before us the qualities of a holy woman of God. To Mary Glenn, my other mother, who provided guidance and friendship during a critical time in my life and spiritual journey. You are a strong mother and dear friend. Thank you for always being there for me and encouraging me through the victories and especially through the tough times. I love you mom.

Finally, to the Women of Macedonia Baptist Church—you are my inspiration for writing this book. Thank you for the joy of being your bible teacher, sister in Christ, and co-laborer in the ministry of the Gospel of Jesus Christ. Through every struggle, hardship, trial, and triumph, God is still working miracles! Always remember this as we continue to learn, serve, and grow together:

*Do you think anyone is going to be able to drive a wedge between us and Christ's love for us? There is no way! Not trouble, not hard times, not hatred, not hunger, not homelessness, not bullying threats, not backstabbing, not even the worst sins listed in Scripture: They kill us in cold blood because they hate you. We're sitting ducks; they pick us off one by one. None of this fazes us because Jesus loves us. I'm absolutely convinced that nothing—nothing living or dead, angelic or demonic, today or tomorrow, high or low, thinkable or unthinkable—absolutely nothing can get between us and God's love because of the way that Jesus our Master has embraced us.*

*Romans 8:35-39, MSG*

# Foreword

The silent pain of women makes one of the loudest sounds in the church. The pain of some women is due to their inability to get over their past. Some women's sorrow is lived out in the context of a marriage to a man who is no less than a fool. There are other women whose distress emanates from battles with inner voices, tragic sexual abuse from within the family circle, the impact of childlessness on her self-esteem, or the challenge of embracing her destiny. The aching hearts of women, however, need not remain silent.

Dr. Linda Colbert has written a powerful work that takes women's pain off the mute and gives women a voice of victory. In "The Struggles of Unloved Women," she brings the stories of women in antiquity to life. She successfully achieves this feat through her selection of stories of women in Scripture who experienced and overcame significant struggles. She opens up the doors to these women's lives in Scripture and allows the reader to look inside. The sights and sounds of pain and difficulty will uniquely resonate with each reader. Most significantly, you will be helped, healed, delivered, equipped, and empowered by what you read and experience. Each chapter is written with revelatory insight, practical application, and thought provoking questions for personal reflection or group study.

*Foreword*

Let God and Dr. Colbert show you how much you are loved and how lovable you really are. Get ready to write a new chapter in your story.

Claybon Lea, Jr., Ph.D., D.Min.
Senior Pastor, Mount Calvary Baptist Church
Fairfield, California

# Introduction

*"I have told you these things that in me you may have peace"*
*(John 16:33).*

One day, while out sharing our faith in Christ, we knocked on a door and a young woman answered. She had a small child with her. He held on to her leg and reached up to me, so I stooped and began to play with his hands. The young woman smiled as if it took some effort and said, "I had a feeling someone was coming to my door today." I introduced myself, told her why we knocked on her door and asked her, "If she was to die today would she be sure that heaven would be her home?" To which she replied, "No, I'm not sure, but I remember accepting Christ when I was a little girl." At that moment it seemed to me that that was not the right question to ask her. Nevertheless, we proceeded to share Christ with her, invited her to attend our church, thanked her for her time and began to walk away. When I glanced back at her she asked, "Do you know this song?" As I walked back toward her she began to sing, "Jesus said, here I stand won't you please let me in, and you said, I will, but tomorrow." I replied, "Yes, I know the song," so I sang back to her, "Your tomorrow could very well be here today."

When our eyes met, she bowed her head and slowly closed the door. I could hear her son crying as I walked away.

It was very difficult for me to continue to knock on doors that day because of the burden I felt for that young woman. I was struck by two things: First, I gained an even greater appreciation for Jesus' passion for the poor. Second, I knew that there was a more compelling story behind her door; and I just wanted to offer her a listening ear. Just listen. Since that day, I have made an effort to look beyond the clipboard and the Four Spiritual Laws Booklet in my hands, but rather, attend more to the faces of the people who kindly open their doors and allow us to share with them. Behind the doors, I have seen faces filled with lines of suffering, violence, addictions, shame, poverty, and grief and loss so great, that the light in their eyes has gone out. When the doors open, I listen to voices riddled with sadness, pain, and words of hopelessness and vexation. Some of them believe that nobody really cares!

Most of the people behind these doors are young women with small children; and they are impoverished emotionally, psychologically, physically, and spiritually. Perhaps, they were abandoned themselves as children; they may be victims of sexual abuse, rape, incest or domestic violence. They might have been ostracized by their communities, estranged from their families or maybe some of them have mental infirmities. Whatever the case, there *is* a story behind every door; and, one thing that they all have in common is that they are not alone in their struggles.

No one will be able to sail through this life without experiencing challenges, painful life events, struggles and hardships, betrayals, faith testing, temptations, or traumas. However, the comforting news is that, there are no trials or struggles uncommon to us.

Someone has experienced the same or a similar adversity. Such is the case in the lives of the ten biblical women chosen for this book. The only difference between the women in ancient times and women today *is* time—the period of history in which they lived. Ancient women had some of the same dreams as we have; they had longings as we have; they faced challenges as we have and they even sinned as we do. The difference is that they lived in a dissimilar culture and society, with even more restrictive religious practices, and less protective laws. Yet they all found a way to exist with dignity! Their fortitude, wisdom, and determination enabled them to overcome some of the most challenging trials and overwhelming sufferings one could imagine. Most importantly, the unseen presence of Almighty God guided and protected them while they were in the midst of their struggles.

These women are courageous, heroic women. They ascended above their circumstances and emerged as victors rather than victims! Some traversed through social mores that were not in their favor—and some suffered great loss. Still they persevered, and through their struggles, they all teach us how to be overcomers and survivors! Behind each door are valuable lessons about life and living.

In *The Struggles of Unloved Women,* you are encouraged to journey into the lives of ten historical women who struggled through amazing trials, but came through better, stronger, more enlivened and victorious! Well—most of them did. As each woman tells her story, she teaches us about the amazing wonders and works of God within the struggles of our lives. We may not see the Lord in the flesh, like Mary, his mother, or talk openly with him, like the Samaritan woman, or even walk with him, serve him or eat with him as did Mary Magdalene—but the Lord Jesus is present with us as we walk through the valley experiences of our lives. The Lord is present when we pray. He is with us in the midst of trauma, he feels our shame, he knows rejection; and he knows each of us—intimately. There is not a hair on our head that the Lord is not intricately acquainted with (Luke 12:7). He knows who you are and where you are. Thus, the sweet Psalmist proclaimed, "Where can I go from His Spirit?" (Psalm 139:7). There is no depth, no valley, or any height where God is not present!

The beauty of this book is found in the character and strength of each of these women. They are different personalities; some are queens and some are peasants. Some of them are single, widowed, and some are married. Some are empty and barren, and some are full. Some are virtuous and noble, and some are malicious and evil. They have encountered catastrophic events such as rape, incest, death, betrayal, murder, and piercings of the soul so great, they thought they would never recover! Nevertheless, through every struggle, they found the strength to endure, because God's quiet voice encouraged them to fight on!

Regardless of the eras, culture, laws, or historical events, women have always been a strong, resilient, and a formidable force of humanity! Women have always found their place in the thick of things like war, politics, religion, in ministry, in the home, through childbirth and child rearing, and even human tragedies. You name it; there is not an advent or event in history where women are not present, engaged, dynamic, and essential!

You are invited to enter through the doors and into the lives of these ten women. Perhaps, your story is the same or a similar one. Hear what each one has to say. Allow these exceptional biblical women to encourage you—forewarn you—and teach you where your strength truly comes from! Learn the lessons. Find answers to your most perplexing questions, but most of all, discover for yourself the greatest love that ever lived! He is the water of life—the unseen hand guiding you and protecting you through every circumstance that you encounter. He is an ever-present God. No matter what your struggles—no matter what you encounter—no matter how traumatic the event—you can be sure of this one thing—God loves you and he has already overcome the world! So be of good cheer and enjoy the journey!

# Behind Door One

## The Woman of Samaria: Discovering the Living Water

> The woman said, "I know that Messiah" (called Christ) "is coming. When he comes, he will explain everything to us."
>
> John 4:25

"What are you looking at? I can see you peering at me from behind that curtain!" I yelled at the woman across the road as I picked up my water pot and made my way to the well. It was boiling hot in the noonday sun and I was just not in the mood. It was the time that I traveled to the well to draw water. "If they want nothing to do with me, why are they so interested in my comings and my goings?" I thought. Of course, I am speaking about the people in my town. I have been a target of ridicule, gossip and judgment for as long as I can remember. I have been ostracized, criticized, and rejected. Nobody wants anything to do with me because I am a sinner. Ha! You should see them—the women I mean—clinging to their husbands whenever I pass along the road. Ah yes, but that does not stop the roving eyes of their men from watching me until I fade into the distance. I see them. I can feel their lustful eyes staring at me.

I have been called everything but my real name. You name it—and that is me. I am a harlot, a prostitute, a woman with a sordid past, and even an adulteress. Have I been with men? Yes, I sure have. I am called promiscuous. Do I drink? Yes! Have I ever been drunk? Sure, many times. I have even been labeled a drunkard—and I could run with the best of them! That said, I do have a name—but no one has ever bothered to ask me—"What is your name, dear?" To them, I am anonymous. I am the invisible woman. Whether colloquial or proper language is used, the most judgmental and hurtful label of all is the one that stuck with me the most—"She is a sinner!" Yes, I am, and I probably was the highest-ranking sinner in Sychar—at least that is what the town's people believed.

My life was lived over two-thousand years ago and still today I am called the "unnamed" or "anonymous" woman at the well. I am the Samaritan woman. Who refers to someone by his or her country anyway? "The Samaritan woman?" Get real! Am I proud of my life? I never have been! Nevertheless, in retrospect, I am grateful for everything that happened to me, and I will gladly tell you why. I am the Woman of Samaria, and this is my story.

## My Hometown in Samaria

My story begins in the capital city of Samaria, a little-known place called Sychar. Sychar, situated in the so-called "fat valleys" of the land, was known for its rich soils and hearty vegetation. When Israel journeyed from Egypt to the Promised Land, the tribe of Ephraim settled there. God blessed this glorious land and gave it as an inheritance to the Israelites—God's chosen people. Unfortunately, what God had blessed to be "a crown of glory" turned into a "crown of pride"—a den of drunkenness, licentiousness, idolatry, and riotous living (Isaiah 28:1–7). The wealthy inhabitants abused and exploited the land and its people. Consequently, the Jews harbored a deep contempt toward the Samaritans and characterized Sychar as a "lying" and "drunken" town. Even the priest and prophets were drunkards. Corrupted by their idolatrous practices, they embraced many unholy alliances. The pleasure-seeking rituals of the leaders in Sychar led to pervasive sexual exploitation, murders, and poverty. Thus, it was difficult for anyone, even the most devout person, to live in Sychar without being influenced by its depravity. Sadly, even I was overcome by the wantonness of Sychar.[1]

Temple worship was a significant part of our everyday lives, yet, sin was rampant! Many of us meandered through life without any real purpose, and generations of my people were perishing because we were oblivious to the true meaning of worship. My life is important in that, many women can relate to my story, especially those who have found themselves in similar situations. Yes, many lessons can be learned from not only my past, but also my encounter with the Jewish stranger I met one day at the well.

# My Condition and Condemnation

Samaritans are a mixed-race people. Our ethnic heritage is Jewish, but we intermarried with people outside of our Jewish race. My ancestors were the exiled Israelites who survived the barbarous captivity of the Assyrian Empire. I could tell you horror stories of some of the most wicked and heinous crimes against humans. My ancestors were tortured and brutalized by the unrestrained and vicious treatment of their Assyrian captors. Not only did the Assyrians abuse their captives, they were idol worshippers. The Assyrians believed that every created being had a spiritual nature so they worshipped the moon, sun, animals, waters, and even the storms. Consequently, they imposed their idolatrous practices on the Israelites held in captivity.

The Israelites from the northern kingdom who survived the horrors of Assyrian captivity settled in Samaria and intermarried with the non-Jewish inhabitants of the land. I am a product of that union—a Samaritan—a mixed-race woman—birthed out of the marriages between the exiled Israelites and the pagans who settled in Samaria. Like our ancestors, we abandoned the practice of serving the one true God and embraced the religious practices of the pagans by blending aspects of Judaism with pagan worship. Nevertheless, the one thing that we did not abandon was the Pentateuch, written by the hand of the Patriarch Moses.[2]

Although, there was a clear connection to the Israelites and my Jewish heritage, Samaritans were hated by the Jews. Racial prejudice permeated our society, and I too was negatively impacted by the hostility between the Jews and Samaritans. The Jews regarded the Samaritans as unclean, a threat to the purity of the Jewish race.

Consequently, not only did we suffer from the hostile effects of racism, we had virtually no contact with the Israelites or the Jewish traditions of our ancestors. Still, Jacob's well was a significant part of our daily life. The well was a constant reminder of not only our Jewish heritage, but the Patriarch Joseph's bones were also buried near the same location. This land was significant in that, it was part of the Promised Land given by God to the Israelites, and was a constant reminder of God's unwavering faithfulness to his chosen people![3]

Not only am I a Samaritan, but also a woman. In my culture, women were devalued; the laws did not favor women very much at all. In ancient times, women were considered inferior to men. In fact, prior to the coming of the Messiah, the attitudes toward women had deteriorated to the degree that Jewish rabbis often prayed, "I thank Thee that I am not a woman, a Gentile, or a slave!"[4] In my culture, the religious leaders of that day would rather burn the law than teach them to a woman because they believed that women were unfit for any in depth religious teaching.[5]

Although the mistreatment of women is not as prevalent as in times past, women are still undervalued, and in some cultures, women are regarded as second class. Here is a fact that might shed some light on my plight. In my time, women did not have the financial means to provide for themselves. It was a common practice for marriages to be arranged, in many cases, to protect men and women from impurity, immorality, and any accusations of rape and other inappropriate contact.[6] Unfortunately for women, a man could divorce his wife for any reason—even something as simple or unreasonable as being displeased by her cooking or her appearance. That left many of us out in the cold! If a woman was divorced, she could lose her inheritance, find it difficult to remarry, and end up living in extreme poverty—because she was unable to provide for her basic needs. As a result, her only recourse was to find work, depend on the kindness of others, beg, or even depend on men—and perhaps prostitution for survival.[7] I did what I had to do to survive. Judge for yourself; the women in Sychar certainly did!

Finally, I was an outcast. My community regarded me as a sinner and no one wanted anything to do with me. I was a woman living with a man who was not my husband. Do you know anyone like that? Well, in my time, I was considered an adulteress. I was judged as unworthy to look upon, not to mention, engage in a meaningful conversation. I endured scornful looks and finger pointing. Whenever I was caught in public, people whispered behind my back. Some were even bold enough to hurl mean-spirited comments at me. I was regarded as promiscuous because it was common knowledge that I had been with many men. I was very lonely. The worst punishment of all was being ostracized from my family and my community! I had no friends and longed for fellowship with the other women in the town. I felt like the invisible woman; unloved and undesirable—knowing only the greedy hands of the men who passed me around from one relationship to the next. But, I did have faith. My only comfort was found in the hidden hope in my heart, that one day the Messiah—called Christ—would come and explain everything. In the meantime, I worshipped in the temple at Mount Gerizim.

Like me, many women have lived in isolation because of sin. King Solomon put it this way, "What has been will be again, what has been done will be done again; there is nothing new under the sun" (Ecclesiastes 1:9). Do not consider yourself alone in your plight. Countless women have suffered in loveless relationships out of either a desperate need for love and companionship or survival. Some, as I did, may believe that they have no other alternative but to lease their bodies out for cash, security, and temporary favors. Too many women are suffering spiritually, emotionally, and psychologically—which can lead to destructive relationships that cause a lifetime of heartache. As for me, I allowed myself to be used as an object for pleasure because my life in Sychar was so bitter. Unfortunately, just as I did, many women have yet to realize that the emptiness they feel inside is an unquenchable thirst, which can only be satisfied by the Jewish stranger I met at the well on that blistering day.

## A Broken Woman for a Broken City

When I arose that morning, I did not know that my life would drastically change forever. I was unaware that on this particular day, the providence of God was at work in my life. The Messiah, called Christ, needed to go through Samaria. It is believed that the Lord was compelled to go through Samaria to meet me at the well, especially at the hour he chose. Wells were places for refreshment, community gatherings, and conversations—rarely would one find someone drawing water during the heat of the day![8] Nevertheless, I believe that the Lord knew that he would find me there. But I was not the only reason that the Lord walked through Samaria that day.

For me, this was like any other day. I gathered my water pot and made my way to the well to gather my provisions of water. I was an outcast, so I traveled to the well at a time when I knew that no one else would be there. The other women in Sychar went to the well in the cool of the day. Of course, I was not welcome in their group. As such, I walked to the well sometime around noon. It was scorching hot that day and I could not wait to have a cool drink before I filled my water pot! But unbeknownst to me, I was on a collision course with a man that would give me a drink of the most refreshing—life-changing water one could imagine!

As I drew closer, from a distance, I could see a man sitting at the well. I felt a twinge of annoyance and fear rise up inside me! I paused for a brief moment and thought about what I would say in response to any salutations from him. As I moved even closer to the well, I noticed that this man was not a Samaritan—he was a Jew. That disturbed me even more! When I finally arrived at the well, I ignored him and went about my task. But I felt his eyes on me—watching me. This time, however, the look was very different from the men in times past. Then, he kindly asked me to give him a drink. Many men had spoken to me in the past, but not in this tone. His voice was unlike any voice I have ever heard! I had been asked for favors, for food, for sex, and even for water—but no one spoke to me with this gentle authority. I felt compelled to look at him—so I timidly glanced at him—and dared to have a conversation with this Jewish stranger, who did not know that the people in Sychar wanted nothing to do with me!

When he asked me to give him a drink, I became defensive. My familiar protective walls begin to rise—poised to shield me from any personal attacks. How is it that he, being a Jew, would dare speak to a Samaritan—not to mention a woman—in public even? I fired back, "You are a Jew and I am a Samaritan woman. How can you ask me for a drink?" (John 4:9). Then he said something very peculiar to me, "If you knew the gift of God and who it is that asks you for a drink, you would have asked him and he would have given you living water." "The gift of God and who it is that asks me for a drink?" His words stung me—my heart began to beat so forcefully and rapidly, I thought even he could hear it! I must have this living water, I thought, but how do I get it from him? My desire for this water was so overwhelming I pressed him cautiously and said, "Sir, you have nothing to draw with and the well is deep. Surely you are not greater than our father Jacob who gave us the well, and drank from it himself!" He said to me, "Everyone who drinks this water will be thirsty again, but whoever drinks the water I give him will never thirst. Indeed, the water I give him will become in him a spring of water welling up to eternal life." I listened with great interest. I had to have this water, for this man was like no man I have ever known. I tried, but I found no way to manipulate him. Although I was fully clothed—I felt naked as I stood before him. I perceived that he knew everything. Perhaps, he was a prophet. Nevertheless, my desire not to come to the well again was so intense I blurted out, "Sir, give me this water so that I won't get thirsty and have to keep coming here to draw water." He answered me with a request, "Go, call you husband and come back." I paused for a moment and said, "I have no husband." His eyes were penetrating when he looked at me again and said, "You are right when you say you have no husband. The fact is, you have had five husbands, and the man you now have is not your husband" (John 4:18). Then, without any condemnation or harsh criticisms, he looked straight through me—opened the book of my life and began to read my story. Nothing was hidden from him. How did he know all that I had ever done? I felt ashamed, yet relieved somehow, as I stood and listened to him expound on all the deep, dark secrets that I thought

I would take to my grave. In truth, he was the only one who really knew my name!

I put forth my best effort to distract him away from speaking about my lifestyle—so I used worship as a point of contention. I knew that the Jews despised the Samaritans for worshiping on Mount Gerizim—for the Jews believed that Jerusalem was the place for worship (John 4:19). Oh, but the Jewish stranger was shrewder than I thought. His wisdom was beyond anything I have ever known. He explained the true meaning of worship and this is what he said:

> Believe me, woman, a time is coming when you will worship the Father neither on this mountain nor in Jerusalem. You Samaritans worship what you do not know; we worship what we do know, for salvation is from the Jews. Yet a time is coming and has now come when the true worshipers will worship the Father in spirit and truth, for they are the kind of worshipers the Father seeks. God is spirit, and his worshipers must worship in spirit and in truth (John 4:21–24).

I was stunned as he opened my eyes to the meaning of true worship. My soul was flooded with hope. The fortified walls that I had built around me began to crumble. The Jewish stranger spoke of all that I had waited for—longed for—and hoped for. He told me that God is not confined to temples and objects, or even religious rituals and ceremonies. God is much greater than that! God is a Spirit, he is invisible, and one cannot touch God with human hands—only with the heart! True worship happens when God's

Spirit joins my frail, thirsty spirit; it is an inward connection, not confined to the temple at Mount Gerizim or even the synagogue in Jerusalem. I can worship God in spirit and truth—wherever I am. I was overwhelmed and enlightened by what he said. Still there was a twinge of fear present as I tried to reason within my heart words too amazing grasp. I wanted to trust him. I wanted to believe—so I said to him, "I know that Messiah "is coming" (who is called Christ). When he comes he will tell us all things." To which he replied, "I who speak to you am he." (John 4:25–26 NKJV). I was beside myself! Could this be true? I fell to the ground on my knees, humbly looked up at him, and I rejoiced! The load of despair I had carried for so long was finally lifted. I felt liberated. I felt the shame and guilt that weighed me down roll away. Like broken chains, the burdens I carried for so long just fell off and rolled away.

Then, there came upon us other Jewish men, but they said nothing. With sheer abandonment, I left my water pot, and I ran as fast as I could into Sychar and cried out, "Come, see a man who told me all things I had ever did! Could this be the Christ?" (John 4:29). They did! The whole town came out and made their way to the well toward the Messiah. When they saw him and heard his words, many of the Samaritans believed and urged Jesus to stay with us. Jesus remained in Samaria for two days and in that time, he transformed a broken, lying, and drunken town into a spiritually enlightened city. I was not the only one in Sychar who was broken; the entire city was broken and for as long as I can remember, I was the dumping ground for their pain.

When Christ came to Samaria, he delivered the entire city. No one can enter into the presence of God and remain the same. After the Samaritans heard his voice, they said to me, "We no longer believe just because of what you said; now we have heard for ourselves, and we know this man really is the Savior of the world" (John 4:42). Sychar needed a Savior. When the Messiah came to Samaria that day, he explained everything to us. He gave us a new perspective on worship and delivered an entire city from the bondage of sin.

## The Lessons

Jesus took time to talk to me. In fact, my conversation with Jesus is one of the longest conversations recorded in the Bible. Jesus came to liberate women from their base status, to positions of honor—not condemn them. My condition was important to Jesus for two reasons: First, Jesus wanted to change my life by revealing the truth to me. For so long I had been blinded by lies and half-truths about my faith, religiosity, and especially my worth. The peoples in Sychar looked on me with scorn and hatred, not because of my sin or who I was, but because they could see a reflection of themselves in me. They were afraid to own the depravity they saw in themselves. But Jesus looked on me with love and compassion—something that I needed to feel for a long time. Second, Jesus wanted to use my testimony as an instrument to bring salvation to the Samaritans in my town. I was ashamed of my life; weakened by it even. But Jesus showed me how to transform my shame into a vessel, which could pour living water into the broken hearts of other thirsty women.

In many ways, your life may parallel my life. You may be ashamed of your past, feel worthless, or even afraid of being rejected by others—just as I was rejected. However, behind the closed doors of your life there is a story to tell. You have a testimony that can tear down the walls of shame and guilt that has held so many women in bondage. God can use your life in the same way that he used my life. You see, two-thousand years later my story is still being told!

What Jesus did that day at the well, was use the life of an anonymous Samaritan woman—with a scandalous past—to turn a broken city upside down. Sychar was as damaged as I was. The entire town lived in darkness. The people in Sychar spent so much time pointing the finger at me, they were unaware of their own shameless condition. They sought to cover their sin by magnifying my sins. But Jesus shined the light on all of the darkness in Sychar. The Lord used the truth to transform a broken city. Now I know—there is a fountain—and it is filled with the water of life. If you drink from that fountain, you will never thirst again!

## Jesus Christ is the Water of Life

If you are thirsty, come and drink from the water of life. Jesus said, "If a man is thirsty, let him come to me and drink. Whoever believes in me, as the Scripture has said, streams of living water will flow from within him" (John 7:37–38). The emptiness that we feel on the inside can only be filled by the unconditional love of Jesus Christ. For a long time, I thought my security, my worth, and my needs could be met in my relationships with men. Unfortunately, I ended up in one unhealthy and unwholesome relationship after another—none of which could satisfy the emptiness inside my heart. My problems were spiritual; and no human hands or relationships could satisfy the deep longing I had for God. I had a superficial knowledge of God. My worship was guided by the practices and teachings of my people. Then, I met Jesus for myself. When my human spirit connected with his Holy Spirit, all of my burdens rolled away. Jesus taught me the truth about genuine worship. Genuine worship leads to authentic living and my life was forever changed. Whatever you are looking for—whatever you are longing for—it can only be found in a relationship with the true and living God. Place your trust in Christ; he will fill your life with good things.

## Face the Truth without Fear

Far too many of us are unable to be delivered because we hide from the truth. The Lord said, "If you hold to my teachings, you are really my disciples. Then you will know the truth, and the truth will set you free" (John 8:31–32). We reject the truth because we are afraid of facing who we really are. We are ashamed of our past deeds and fear what people might think of us. Perhaps, you will be judged—especially by those who are afraid themselves of who *they* really are! But you cannot allow yourself to be driven away or shamed out of your deliverance by pious and judgmental critics. The truth empowers us rather than weakens us. Truth is the greatest liberator. Truth is the door that releases us from our heavy and hidden burdens. The truth opens doors so that a wounded person can come out of darkness and into to the light. Truth is the good news about a Savior who can heal, deliver, and set free. How many opportunities have we missed to help a wounded soul find comfort through the love of Christ because we were ashamed of our past? God uses that which was once broken to strengthen those who are living shattered lives. You must not be afraid to share your life's story. Tell others about his goodness! Tell them how he saved you. Proclaim to the meek a testimony of his power. Tell them about his faithfulness and his power to heal. Tell them how you were once dead in sin and trespasses but his love made you alive again. Speak of how he delivered you from darkness and helped you conquer your fears. Tell them about what you know, and not what others have said. Draw those who are lost to Christ with the same thing he drew you with—his truth!

## Transform Your Shame into a Ministry

You do not have to be crippled by your past. Just as countless women have given their hearts and lives to Jesus Christ, you too can do the same. Once you receive forgiveness, you no longer have to carry the weight of the sins from your past. Your past mistakes were nailed to an old rugged cross over two-thousand years ago. Now, you can use them as an instrument of healing and empowerment rather than a load of weakness, guilt, and low self-worth. Jesus told me everything that I had ever done. I could not deny it because nothing is hidden from God. Confess your sins and be healed. Once you have been converted, you must strengthen your sisters! That is how you transform your shame into a ministry. It takes courage to acknowledge your faults and confess your sins. Yet the only way to change your circumstances is to agree with God that you are a sinner and you need to be saved. Then, you must accept his forgiveness and not allow yourself to sink back into the dark hole of shame and guilt from which you have been delivered.

## Study Questions

1. What were the struggles faced by the Samaritan woman, and how do the same struggles influence today's women?
2. How did the people in Sychar treat the Samaritan woman? How did Jesus treat her?
3. Have you known women who have endured the same treatment as the Samaritan woman? How would you treat such a woman?
4. What do you think would have happened to the Samaritan woman if the women in Sychar had encouraged and embraced her, rather than judge and reject her? (Galatians 6:1–2).
5. How did racism and sexism negatively affect the Samaritan woman's life?
6. In looking at the life of the Samaritan woman, how does one's environment play a role in one's decision-making and lifestyle?
7. What did Jesus say to the Samaritan woman that convinced her that he was more than a prophet?
8. The values toward women in ancient Israel were different than they are today. In what ways have the church evolved in its treatment of women?
9. What insight have you gained about the way Jesus viewed women in ancient times?
10. What principles about true worship have you learned from the Samaritan woman's story and how will this study influence your future commitment to worship?

# Behind Door Two
## Abigail: When Beauty Marries a Fool

> "Now think it over and see what you can do, because disaster is hanging over our master and his whole household. He is such a wicked man that no one can talk to him."
>
> 1 Samuel 25:17

I was stunned when the servant rushed in and said, "David sent messengers from the desert to give our master his greetings, but he hurled insults at them." "What?" I said. Nabal had no idea what he had done. My legs nearly gave out on me as I listened to the servant's report. Nabal had done it again but this time he had gone too far. I have made excuses for his ill-mannered remarks and insensitive words on so many occasions. How can someone be so brutish and hateful? Nabal was the rudest, most ill-tempered, and mean-spirited man I had ever known. Nevertheless, he was my husband and it was my duty to make his home a house of peace.

True to his name, Nabal was a fool. He had foolishness wrapped up in his thinking and his actions, and he showed no remorse for any of the damage that he caused others. In all the time Nabal and I were married, I never witnessed an apology for anything that he said. He was so arrogant. There were times when I could sense a hint of regret, but Nabal was so prideful, he would blame others for his actions. Well, people like Nabal who refuse to change are on a fast track to a horrible end. That is exactly what happened to Nabal. With all of his wealth and his potential to do well, he squandered his life on cynicism, drunkenness, stubbornness, and foolishness. But this time, he brought disaster upon all of us!

What could I do? With haste, I gathered loaves of bread, raisins, and skins of wine. I prepared a peace offering for David and his men. In a panic, I said to the servants, "Dress five sheep and gather the grain, cakes, and figs. Hurry! Load the donkeys and rush ahead of me; I will follow you. Maybe we can intercept him before he destroys all of us. Go quickly! I will meet you in the ravine. Perhaps my lord will have mercy and repent of the evil he plans for us." I said nothing to Nabal. As I rushed to the desert, I rehearsed what I would say to David and his men. When I saw David, I lighted off my donkey and bowed down with my face to the ground. I was so frightened my body trembled. "Please, my lord, let the blame fall on me!" I cried. Then I stood and told David all that was in my heart. I struggled to maintain my composure. When I finally had the courage to look on his face, I was amazed by what I saw in his eyes. Then he spoke. I am Abigail, and this is my story.

## The Place and Predicament

It was right after the prophet Samuel died when things began to change for me. All the people were mourning Samuel's death. It was a sad time for Israel. After a period of great mourning, Samuel was buried with our Fathers at his home in Ramah. Samuel was a noble and honorable prophet and his death represented a great loss for Israel. He was only a boy when his mother dedicated him to serve in the temple under Eli the priest. After Eli and his sons died, God called Samuel as the priest and the last judge of Israel (1 Samuel 2:11). Samuel was beloved—he was upright and gentle in spirit. He was nothing like Eli and his wicked sons, Hophni and Phinehas.

It was a very tumultuous time for Israel. We were constantly at war with the Philistines, and David, the son of Jesse, was on the run. King Saul was trying to kill David, so he fled to the mountains. At first, no one really understood why David was on the run. After all, David was one of King Saul's most loyal and mighty warriors. But Saul and his men pursued David and tried on many occasions to kill him. Some people said Saul was jealous of David and his jealously drove him insane. Others believed that Saul sought to kill David because he feared that David would become Israel's next king. As it turns out, both reports were true. Unfortunately, King Saul found out in the most dreadful way that no one has the power to overthrow God's plans. It was a tragedy when King Saul and his sons, especially David's friend Jonathan, died at the hands of the Philistines!

David and his men, about 600 of them, were hiding in the Desert of Maon. Our home in Carmel was not far from there. Maon was a desert place in the mountainous region of Judah. There was plenty of room for flocks and herds of many kinds to graze there. Nabal was a wealthy man. His land spread across a substantial part of the wilderness of Maon. He had many servants and possessed many flocks and sheep; but we had no children.

Nabal was a descendant of Caleb—the son of Jephunneh—but you would not have known it (Numbers 14:30). Caleb was a faithful servant of the Lord and a brave soldier. When Moses sent the ten spies to investigate the Promised Land, only Joshua and Caleb returned with a good report. Because of this, they were the only two men over the age of twenty years old to enter into the Promised Land (Numbers 14:29–30). When the time was right, the Lord gave Caleb great strength to subdue the sons of Anak and take the rich vast land of Hebron for himself and his clan. Caleb was eighty-years old when he took the land from the inhabitants of Hebron (Judges 1:20). God gave him strength and Caleb enjoyed the wealth of the land until he went on to sleep with our Fathers. Nabal, being a Calebite, inherited his ancestor's estate.[1]

## The Challenges of Living with a Foolish Husband

In my culture, the parents often arranged marriages. As a result, there were few options for a woman if she was given in marriage to a man like Nabal. Nabal inherited his wealth from Caleb—but he did not inherit Caleb's character. Nabal was a brutish drunkard. He was overindulgent, hateful and churlish—and that made it difficult to live with him. With all that he possessed, he never realized that a noble character is much more desirable than wealth. It is written in the Proverbs, *Wise men store up knowledge, but the mouth of a fool invites ruin.* My husband's life and premature death is a testament to this proverb—for his mouth was indeed his undoing.

The quality of a person is not measured by his or her wealth or found in the abundance of possessions. An honorable character is worth far more than rubies (Proverbs 31:10). Thus, the quality of our character is what makes us wealthy. Nabal was a wealthy man but he was worthless! Like me, you might be married to a man like Nabal. Nevertheless, I did not allow Nabal's character to determine the manner in which I responded to him. It was never my place to try to change him. My words and actions toward Nabal were always as unto the Lord. For whatever we do in word or deed must be done in the name of the Lord with thanksgiving (Colossians 3:17). A virtuous woman is one who does good and not evil to her husband. We must obey God and submit to our husbands according to God's Word—not according to our husband's character. We must remain gracious and committed to our marriage vows and trust that God will be faithful, no matter what our circumstances may be.

## A Fool's Response to Kindness

It was sheep-shearing time when one of the servants rushed in and said, "Nabal has insulted David and his men!" Nabal had spoken harsh words to many people, but this time was like no other. David and his men had moved to the Desert of Maon. While there, they showed kindness toward the shepherds. They watched over them and protected them from the Philistines who, if given the chance, would have robbed the threshing floors, and then moved on to plunder the sheepfolds (1 Samuel 23:1). Night and day, David's men stood guard and protected the shepherds (1 Samuel 25:16). While in the wilderness, David and his men ate what they hunted and killed. They had very few provisions, but they took nothing for themselves from Nabal's men—not even a lamb. This is remarkable because David's men were outcasts and rebels. They were discontented men who owed debts and had very few necessities. They were desperate renegades and could have used violence to take whatever they wanted. But they took on David's spirit and proved loyal to his instructions. Instead of violence, these men showed kindness toward the shepherds—and did them no harm.

Great leaders can turn renegades and nonconformists into trustworthy loyalists who do good rather than evil. David was such a man. He modeled virtues of truth and commitment before his men. He gave them a sense of purpose and pride. David brought out what was good in the men that aligned themselves to him. That is why I was sorely vexed when told what Nabal had done.

As I listened to the servant's report, it was clear to me that Nabal had caused grave damage to not only to himself, but also to everything that he owned. When David sent his men to ask Nabal for provisions, he carefully instructed them on what to say—for he knew that if he humbled himself before the owner, surely, he would grant his request. He expected Nabal to be a reasonable man. After all, they protected Nabal's shepherds without asking for anything in return.

The timing could not have been better. It was a festive time, and Nabal had plenty to celebrate. He always celebrated during this time. He was a man of good fortune, and as in times past, he was shearing thousands of sheep and goats. It was only reasonable for Nabal to show kindness toward David and his men by honoring their request for provisions. He certainly had more than enough to share. But true to his character, Nabal was harsh towards David's men. He insulted them and answered them roughly. He even denigrated David and his family and sent the men on their way with nothing! Still, the men restrained themselves from doing harm to Nabal—they all returned to tell the matter to David.

## My Wisdom and Intercession

I had to move with haste if there was any hope of escaping the impending disaster that Nabal brought on us because of his foolish talk. Even the shepherds knew that Nabal's words were hostile and detestable. His behavior towards David and his men was inexcusable! But in times like these, one must consider the need for action, and I had to weigh these events very carefully.

This was a delicate matter. I had to find a way to atone for the deeds of a foolish man in order to preserve the life of the innocent. I told Nabal nothing about my plans because I knew that in his drunken condition, he would not listen to reason. So I packed hundreds of loaves of bread, wine, cakes of raisins, and figs. I instructed the servants to quickly dress five sheep and load them on top of the donkeys (I Samuel 25:18). It was an offering for Nabal. For me, it was a sacrifice to atone for his sin. My hope was in God's divine providence and I trusted that God would move on the heart of his servant David. After all, the people thought of him as the sweet psalmist with a loving heart towards God's people. If David were true to his character, surly he would have mercy on us.

I believe that God is present in every situation that we face. He knows what we need and although we cannot see him, he is always there. I held on to this belief and so must you. You must trust in

God no matter what you face. Was I afraid? Yes I was. Did I have doubts? Of course I did! Yet through it all, God gave me favor. It took courage—but a major catastrophe was prevented because of the wisdom the Lord provided at that moment. He will do the same for any woman that finds herself in the predicament that I had the misfortune to experience.

Far too many women become cynical and even bitter when they are married to foolish men. Unfortunately, that attitude is very destructive and certainly not the answer. We must never wage war against our husbands by becoming vindictive or resentful. God did not intend for us to be that way. We are all responsible for our attitudes and behaviors. Since God is our Creator, we must identify with him, and not our husbands. We must pursue every opportunity to emulate the qualities and character of God—no matter what.

Humility is a virtue not a weakness. It is a godly characteristic to be desired rather than despised. We are never more precious in the sight of the Lord, than when we possess a meek and humble spirit (1 Peter 3:4). The women of old embraced these qualities rather than viewing them as a sign of weakness. They were godly women who taught us to trust God and never neglect our duties as wives and servants of the Most High. We must practice these principles, regardless of the times in which we live. A humble spirit must be embraced with joy and an obedient heart—for what we do is unto the Lord. When we do so, our families will be blessed and our homes will be a peaceful sanctuary.

## God's Divine Intervention

When I made my way to the mountain ravine, I saw David and his men heading straight towards me. I lighted off my donkey and bowed my face so low to the ground that I could almost breathe in the dust! I heard the snorts of the horses and I could feel David and his men as they encircled me. When I stood to face David, he was nothing like I imagined. "Please let your servant speak to you; hear what your servant has to say." I hurriedly said.

David listened as I explained. Everyone was silent as I pleaded my case. I told David of the kind of man Nabal was with as much dignity as I could express in such a dire situation. I entreated him not to waste revenge on such a fool! I reminded David of the kind of man *he* was—a man of honor—with no evil found in him. I reminded David of all the times that God had avenged him from the wrongs that he suffered and I convinced him that God would avenge him of the affront committed by Nabal too. David listened carefully as I appealed to his conscience. Then an amazing thing happened. He blessed me for my wisdom and good judgement and thanked God for keeping him blameless from yet another offense. David graciously repented of the destruction he planned for Nabal and all that he owned. He took my gift and sent me on my way. As I made my way back home, I was exhausted. I dreaded facing Nabal; I hoped that he would be asleep.

## The Day Nabal's Heart Failed

The next morning when I entered into Nabal's room, he was sober—but he was still groggy from all of the wine he drank the night before. When I approached Nabal, he reached out his hand to pull me to himself. He smelled of the drunken odor of the night's gluttony and merriment. His hair was knotty and dampened with sweat—and he had dried food in his beard. But this time was not as other times. Nabal's face grew sullen as I approached him. It was as if he felt ashamed. I cannot describe what I saw in him that morning, but he listened as I sat next to him and began to speak.

It had been a long time since Nabal had given heed to a word that I said to him. But on this particular morning, he was very attentive. I could feel God's presence with me as I began to share with Nabal the events of the night before. Nabal seemed to have an abundance of favor on earth; he was wealthy—he was in charge—and he believed he could do whatever he wanted. Unfortunately, he paid no attention to his soul. He ignored the fact that every living soul has to depart this body and face an eternal destination. Consequently, Nabal was not prepared for what happened next.

I told Nabal about David and his men—how they had kept watch over the shepherds and protected them from the pillages of the Philistines. I explained to him that David was a loyal and devoted servant of King Saul and that he and his men had been holding up in the strongholds in the Desert of Maon. I stressed to Nabal that David and his men took nothing from him, not even one lamb. They respected his property, guarded his men and lived off what they hunted for themselves (I Samuel 25:37). I told Nabal how David and his men did nothing but good and he repaid them with evil. I told him that David armed his men with swords, about 400 of them, and that they were sure to destroy him and all of his possessions. Then—I told him what I did!

When I told Nabal all that was in my heart, he withdrew within himself. Nabal's face was like a stone and he hardly spoke a word. For the next several days, Nabal was depressed. Perhaps he thought about the life he had lived. Maybe he realized how his drunkenness and self-indulgence had robbed him of a life with purpose and meaning. I would like to think that Nabal was sorry for what he had done. But for all the days that I lived with him and hoped that he would change, Nabal never so much as showed a hint of remorse for the life he lived. Nabal had so much, but yet so little—all because of his foolhardiness. In ten days, the Lord required his soul, and Nabal died a wealthy fool!

## The Lessons

My story is not about Nabal's foolishness as much as it is about my commitment to an ungodly husband. What must a woman do if she finds herself in the same or a similar predicament? Nabal was a fool by name; and for most of his life, he was overindulgent and stingy. Worst of all, he was an unbeliever—and it was difficult to live with an unbelieving husband. As in my case, some women married an unbelieving husband through no fault of their own. Still others chose to marry an unbelieving husband through willful acts of disobedience. Regardless of the circumstances of our marriages, we must remain true to our marriage vows; for in doing so, we honor God. Remember, the vows that we make are unto the Lord— and it is better not to make a vow, than to make one and not fulfill it (Ecclesiastes 5:5). Rather than becoming bitter or trying to find a way of escape, we must live like the holy women of the past. These women adorned themselves with inner beauty. They were intelligent, wise, submissive to their husbands, and they had a meek and quiet spirit. They witnessed to their husbands with their chaste and godly conduct and won them over without a word (1 Peter 3:4).

God teaches us great lessons through hardships and struggles. Did I feel unloved? Yes, at times I did. But I held on to the great love and abundant grace that God granted to me every day that I spent with Nabal. God kept me from sin, and so I tried to find ways to glorify him, even in the midst of a difficult marriage.

## The Blessings of a Godly Influence

There is the tendency to believe that Nabal got just what he deserved. But nothing could be further from the truth. A man like Nabal is in need of great compassion. Nabal was labeled at birth and destined to be a fool—because his name meant "fool." A name can have so much power. Names often define our behavior, temperament, and even our character. Therefore, we must be careful when choosing a name for our children. Abigail means "Father of Joy" or "Cause of Joy."[2] A father's joy brings delight and happiness to a home. The loveliest qualities of a woman are found in her inner beauty—not her outward appearance. Wisdom is much more to be desired than outward beauty because wisdom comes from God. Wisdom reveals traits in women, such as grace and piety, intelligence and gentleness. It teaches us to respond to difficult circumstances and difficult people with tact and discretion, rather than rudeness or aggressiveness. A beautiful woman is one who possesses wisdom, intelligence, loveliness, and humility. To be sure, physical attractiveness has its place. But Humility, gentleness, meekness and obedience—these qualities are essential to godliness and make us beautiful on the inside and on the outside.

God's Word teaches us that a woman with a meek and quiet spirit is very precious in the sight of God (1 Peter 3:4). The truest measure of a woman's sanctification is found in her willingness to obey God. Remember, you might be the only sacred book that your husband reads, or the only light that can show him the way out of darkness. Position yourself to be the instrument God uses to lead an unbelieving husband to a saving knowledge of the Lord Jesus Christ (1 Peter 3:1).

## The Blessings of Submission

Perhaps some might believe that it was unwise to submit to a drunken, ill-tempered, and boorish man like Nabal. Still others might go as far as calling me "the fool." Let me share with you a little about my culture. We did not have "Women's Liberation," "Womanism," "Feminism," or movements as you have in your culture. Women were not esteemed in high regard until after the Messiah came and put things back in order. In ancient Jewish culture, women remained in their father's house until they married. Often, these marriages were arranged and in some cases arranged from birth.[3] And so, marriages were not always built on love, mutual admiration, and respect. My desire to submit to Nabal came from an inward desire to submit to God. Everything that I did for Nabal and for my household came from my devotion and reverent fear of Almighty God.

Holy women of God submit themselves to the Lord and they obey him rather than man (Colossians 3:17–18). A gracious and godly attitude strips away the pride that brings shame to a Christian household. When we live in obedience and humbly submit our lives to God, he will strengthen us and give us the wisdom and fortitude to bear our burdens. Nabal was wicked and mean-spirited, but I submitted myself to him as his wife and helper (Ephesians 5:24). I knew that if he did not change, his outcome would be disastrous. Oh, how I longed to see the day when Nabal would come to know the Lord as I knew him. I never wanted Nabal to live out his days as an ill-tempered foolish man. I desired what was best for Nabal, but Nabal had to desire that too! We cannot justify our negative attitudes or quarrelsome and ill-mannered behaviors by blaming other people. It is, however, our duty to obey God and leave all the battles to the Lord. That is the heart of a godly woman—a woman of wisdom and inner beauty.

## The Blessings of Knowing God

My marriage to Nabal was challenging at best. However, that does not mean that I was not content. My contentment was found in my relationship with the Lord, which is the final lesson you must learn. When the Lord is your God, you can experience joy and peace—even in the midst of the most challenging and bitter circumstances. My days began and ended with spending precious time with God. He alone was my joy; and so, for me, taking care of Nabal was never a chore. Oh yes, there were times when I was frustrated and lonely. I suppose Nabal loved me in his own way. But a man must first possess God's love in his own heart. Only then will he be able to love his wife as God intended. Remember, an unbelieving husband is incapable of expressing the kind of sacrificial love needed in a godly a marriage (Ephesians 5:25).

Were there moments of weakness on my part? Yes! But in those moments of weakness, I found strength in the Lord. I cultivated a relationship with the Lord. I worshiped him and prayed without ceasing. Throughout the day, I lifted up prayers, psalms of praise and thanksgiving. In every chore, I thought of the Lord and meditated on the words of the prophets and seers. I may not have been able to touch God, but his presence was felt everywhere—in the trees—vast lands—the wind—God was always near. Most of my life was centered on God, and that is how I was able to be a good wife to Nabal.

God hears the cries of our hearts. When we seek him, he hears and answers. In everything, the good and the bad, I remained faithful to God, and I held on to every promise. When your circumstances are difficult you must remember that God is with you. If you are married to a foolish man like Nabal, do not be bitter. Let your chaste and gracious conduct abide in your home. Resist the temptation to become angry, bitter, or vengeful. My life is a testament to the fact that the Holy and Divine God sees and knows your plight. He will rescue you and your latter days will be your best!

## Study Questions

1. What is the meaning of Abigail's name? How is her name reflected in her character?
2. How did the culture and times influence Abigail's marriage to Nabal?
3. What type of man was Nabal and in what ways did his name reflect his character?
4. What are some of the challenges Abigail faced in her marriage to Nabal? How did she overcome them?
5. What are some of the challenges faced by todays Christian women who marry an unbelieving husband?
6. Why was it important for Abigail to submit to Nabal? (Ephesians 5:24).
7. What lessons does Abigail teach us about inner beauty and outward beauty? What character traits should women pursue?
8. In light of Abigail's life, what should one consider when choosing a mate?
9. How did God reward Abigail's piety and faithfulness toward her godless husband?
10. In what ways did Abigail's atonement for Nabal's sin resemble Christ's atonement for the sins of man?

# 3

# Behind Door Three
## Mary Magdalene: From Demons to Devotion

"Woman," he said, "why are you crying? Who is it you are looking for?" . . . "Do not hold on to me, for I have not yet returned to the Father. God instead to my brothers and tell them, 'I am returning to my Father and your Father, to my God and your God.'"

John 20:15–17

It was damp and very cold that night. I was crouched in a corner in the back of an alley. There was trash everywhere—rats, roaches, smelly dried food, what a nasty pit! I saw shadows in the darkness. I was so afraid. The voices were back screaming, "Get away from me or I will kill you!" The voices were always angry and distressing. They screamed at me again, "Kill him—kill him!" In a fit of anger, I cupped my ears and cried out, "Somebody please . . . stop the screaming! Stop the howling animals—please stop yelling at me, I cannot bear it anymore. Please, stop the voices." Then the laughter and mocking started. "Stop laughing at me... who is it?" I asked. The voices shouted back, "You are no good—get away from me or I will kill you!"

My feet were cold and dirty. "Where are my shoes?" I whispered. I was soaking wet. Trembling from the cold, I looked around. I had no idea where I was, or how I got here. Just as at other times, I had lost track of the time. "How long has it been this time?" I wondered. Sometimes, I would go to bed at night in the comfort of my home, and I wake up the next morning in a field—wet from the dew. There were times when I would roam the streets, sometimes for days. "How did I get here? Who brought me to this place?" I would always ask the same questions. But there were never any answers. Ashamed, afraid, and confused, I would gather myself and run home. "Will it ever end?" I cried out in distress. The children—oh, the children could be so cruel. They would laugh at me—throw rocks at me—and call me "Crazy Lady!" They would taunt me, "Hey, crazy lady!" I would yell back at them, "Stop it! Get away from me you children of Belial!" Then, they would mock me and run away. Everybody laughed at me. The people in Magdala thought I was crazy—they were all afraid of me. Some would look at me and point fingers at me, as if I was some kind of an animal. "I am not an animal or some sort of aberration!" I am Mary Magdalene, and this is my story.

## The Mystery of My Identity

I am called Mary Magdalene because I was born in Magdala. Magdala is a wealthy port city located on the northwest shore of the

Sea of Galilee, just south of Capernaum. The name Magdala means "Fish Tower" which relates to the many towers used to salt and stack fish for preservation. Magdala was a very prosperous town. The economy was built on commercial fishing and it was a mecca for the dye works and the textile industry. There were many factories in Magdala; most people lived well. I had a very comfortable life there as well.[1]

There is a lot of mystery surrounding my identity. No one knows much about my ancestry or upbringing. Sadly, some have accused me of being a sinful woman with a terrible reputation. I am not sure which is worse, being insane or living in sin! Nevertheless, I have been accused of being many things, including an adulteress and a prostitute.[2] Some have confused me with the woman who was caught in the act of an adulterous encounter (John 8:3). No, I am not that woman. She was half-naked when an angry mob of the Pharisees threw her in the temple court—right at Jesus' feet. Their only motive was to entrap Jesus. That behavior was reprehensible! Still others have accused me of being the woman that Jesus met at Jacob's well in Samaria (John 4). That is not who I am. In fact, I am ashamed to admit that like most Jews, I avoided Samaria as much as I possibly could. Besides, my hometown, Magdala, is north of Samaria. I have never lived in Samaria, nor have I been married five times. I am accused of being the woman that crashed Simon the Leper's party (Matthew 26). Now that was classic! That woman was so courageous as she walked through a sneering crowd of men—took an alabaster jar of spikenard—very expensive perfume—and anointed Jesus. Her worship was something to be envied. She even washed Jesus' feet with her tears. To be sure, I would have given anything to have that moment with Jesus. She showed more love and gratitude than the host Simon did; even though Jesus healed Simon from leprosy. Finally, some have accused me of being a fallen woman, and portrayed me as some mythical goddess, including the Lord's secret wife, and the mother of his children![3] But the truth is, I am a sinner, saved only by the grace of God! I am Mary of Magdala, the one out of whom seven demons were cast out.

## My Struggle with Demonic Possession

I was tormented by demons. My affliction caused me to suffer from bouts of insanity. At times, I was delusional and I trusted no one. The loneliness, anxiety, rejection, and abuse were the worst of it. I cannot tell you very much about what it was like—most of it is a blur. Nevertheless, demonic possession is absolute torture for anyone misfortunate enough to be invaded by this evil. I really do not remember much about what happened when the demons took control, except to say, that sometimes I heard angry voices screaming at me and telling me to do some of the vilest things imaginable! It was an excruciatingly dark period in my life. I was confused. Sometimes I felt like a wild beast! I would wake up in some of the oddest places—dazed and disoriented—not remembering how I got there, or how long I had been there. I would lose track of time; I could not remember days or even weeks of my life. The loneliness was unbearable. I had no friends or family. I was afraid of people, and they were afraid of me. Sometimes I wandered the streets for days, and there were times, I could not find my way home. I was inside my body, but something else was controlling me; I could not escape it!

## Behind Door Three – Mary Magdalene: From Demons to Devotion

I wish I could tell you when or how I met Jesus. Those details are lost. What I do know is that I was possessed and tortured by demons so powerful that people were horrified by my appearance and unpredictable behaviors. I was not alone. There was a lot of demonic activity in that area and many people were tormented by evil spirits.[4] I remember a man of the region of the Gerasenes who lived in the tombs. He was possessed by so many demons that the demons called themselves "Legion" (Mark 5:9). I had seven demons, but he had legions! That poor man spent his days and nights in the tombs and the hills, roaming around, naked, cutting himself with stones, and crying out (Mark 5:1–10). He had no peace. He was left alone to live in torment. Much like I was. The people in that town tried to restrain him but he was too strong—he could not be controlled (Mark 5:4). In the darkness of the tombs, he cried out in agony. Then one day he met Jesus. Jesus commanded the demons to come out of him and from that day on, he was set free!

Demon possession often mimics illnesses such as, epilepsy, insanity, and even deafness or muteness.[5] Evil spirits are not selective. They can torment anyone—all they need is an open door. Thus, we must take seriously the power of demonic spirits. Some of us were poor, unfortunate victims of satanic influence. Others by virtue of their stubbornness and willful acts of disobedience became vulnerable to demonic possession.

You might be wondering if a believer can be possessed by a demon. Demons have power but that power is limited. When the Lord expels a demon or demons from the person, that person is cleansed forever. However, when we reject Christ or choose to live our lives in rebellion, we become vulnerable for the evil spirits to return and our final condition will be worse than the first (Luke 11:24–26).[6]

Jesus is the great Physician. Unfortunately, man has become his own physician. The Scriptures teach us that the only way a man or woman can keep his or her life pure is to live according to God's Word. When we live for God, he gives us the power to resist the devil's attempts to control our minds and our wills. Remember, we will never be completely healed until we experience a *supernatural*, not superficial, encounter with the Lord Jesus Christ. Once converted, we must be transformed by the renewing of our minds (Romans 12:2).

## My Transformation and Discipleship

There is no greater honor in life than the privilege of serving God. After I was healed, I devoted my life to serving Jesus. I was not alone; several other women followed Jesus during his ministry, many of whom were healed from demons and other diseases. It was a wonderful fellowship of women. There was Joanna, Susanna, and many others. We traveled with Jesus and his disciples—ministering to them—as they spread the good news of the kingdom of God (Luke 8:1–3). The women were close. We used our resources to support Jesus and the disciples as they went from one village to another ministering to the poor. These devout women became Disciples of Christ, and some stood by him when he was crucified.

Out of the depths of every heart should spring forth a fountain of gratitude—f or the Lord has sacrificed so much for our salvation. My commitment, and that of the other disciples, both men and women, was to share the good news of Christ so that no man would be lost. We left our homes and families to join with Christ in his ministry, and unashamedly identified ourselves as servants of the Most High God!

## The Dark Day at the Cross

Jesus warned us of the dark days ahead. The chief priests and teachers of the law were always seeking ways to get rid of Jesus, but they feared the people (Luke 22:2). They tried on many occasions to trap Jesus. But his wisdom was not of our world—for he *was* God. They finally found a way by paying Judas Iscariot, one of the twelve disciples, thirty pieces of silver to betray Jesus. Imagine that. Judas was among Jesus' closest companions. Jesus taught Judas, fed him, laughed with him, and even prayed with him. Judas walked with Jesus and watched the Lord perform many miracles. Jesus called Judas a friend—and even washed his feet! But Satan entered Judas' heart and he betrayed our Lord for thirty coins of silver (Matthew 26:14–16).

Judas was greedy. He was unclean—his motives were not pure—and he opened the door for Satan to gain a place in his heart. Satan is always lurking, seeking whom he may devour. Whenever you are unprepared and not fully armed with Spiritual weapons, you become vulnerable to demonic influence (Ephesians 6:10). After Satan entered Judas's heart, he went to the chief priests and made a deal to betray Jesus (Luke 22:3).

It was an ominous night. My soul was restless and troubled. I was not sure why—I just felt that something bad was going to happen. Looking back, Jesus had already warned us that he would suffer many things by men (Mark 8:31). Perhaps, we all were in denial. It was during the Passover when they arrested the Lord. Jesus was in the Garden of Gethsemane with eleven of his disciples when the officers of the temple guard took him that night. The chief priests questioned him; but he said nothing. They wanted him to tell them if he was the Christ. Some who were present at the trial mocked him and beat him. Finally, someone asked, "Are you the Son of God?" To which Jesus replied, "You are right in saying I am." (Luke 22:70).

They marched Jesus before Pilate and Herod. But they found no fault in him because he was innocent. As time went on, the chief priests and teachers of the law stirred up the people and the mob grew larger, louder, and more unruly! I thought I was hearing angry voices again; I was afraid the demons were coming back. But something inside my heart reassured me that it was only the angry mob. Pontius Pilate tried to reason with the people but they demanded that Jesus be crucified. It was awful. The people were out of control. They had no idea what they were doing. Then, out of sheer exasperation, Pontius Pilate disowned the travesty and granted their demand. Pilate disowned the matter, but he condemned Jesus to be crucified at the will of the people.

We stood among the crowd, watching, as Jesus made his way to the cross. We felt so helpless. We prayed, cried, and held on to each other. We followed Jesus as he carried the cross to Calvary to be crucified. The soldiers beat him, spat on him, and mocked him the whole way. As we walked, I started to remember things like, how it was not that long ago when we were in Galilee. Jesus was so loving and kind when he touched the people—no one was rejected—no need went unmet. How can I reach Him now? He was so bloody!

His mother and I held on to each other—weeping. Then something odd happened. Jesus turned, looked at us and said:

> Daughters of Jerusalem do not weep for me; weep for yourselves and for your children. For the time will come when you will say, 'Blessed are the barren women, the wombs that never bore and the breasts that never nursed!' Then "'they will say to the mountains, "Fall on us!" and to the hills, "Cover us!"' For if men do these things when the tree is green, what will happen when it is dry? (Luke 23:28–31).

He warned us that we should weep for ourselves and for our children, whose sins were the reason for his death. We should weep for the coming calamities and destruction of Jerusalem, for the wrath of God will come, and there will be no escape for this untoward generation. Jesus willingly died for us. Nevertheless, he knew that death could not hold him and that the grave would have no victory over him. The Lord knew that soon, he would be reunited with his Father. The Messiah was with us in the flesh, but we rejected him. Now, we would face many trials and tribulations without his physical presence.[9] Still, even at that dark hour, Jesus had more to give us through his words. He kept on giving when they beat him, when they nailed him, and when they lifted him—Jesus, kept on giving.

When we reached Calvary, we watched the Roman soldiers nail our Lord to the cross. The soldiers were so brutal—they enjoyed humiliating and beating Jesus. For me, it felt like every nail he took was being nailed through my heart. I was trembling and weeping so much, that I could barely see through the tears in my eyes. Perhaps, that was best. By this time, all of the disciples were gone, except John—he stood with us at the cross. The other disciples were so afraid. I had no idea where Peter was. John held on to Mary and tried to comfort her, but there was no comfort at the cross. At first, we stood at a distance; but somehow we ended up at the foot of the cross where Jesus was crucified. It was almost unbearable to look on his face. How Jesus endured the pain, humiliation, taunts, and the suffering is beyond words. He just hung on the cross—bleeding and dying for our sins. It was a redemptive story that I shall never forget. I am a part of that story and so are you.

## My Joy in the Morning Light

It was the first day of the week. I went to the tomb early that morning. It was still dark outside as I walked through the Garden and made my way to Jesus' tomb. When I got there, the stone was rolled away and the tomb was empty. I was horrified. I ran as fast as I could and found Simon Peter and John. I said, "They have taken the Lord out of the tomb, and we don't know where they have put him!" (John 20:2). We all ran back to the Garden. Simon Peter went inside and found Jesus' strips of linen and burial cloth folded neatly inside. But Jesus was not in the tomb. We stood outside, dazed and confused. What did this all mean? Then, the disciples walked away and returned to their homes. I was left standing alone in the garden. I stood outside the tomb and I wept.

After some time passed, I bent over and looked again inside the tomb. Two men were there! How did they get inside? How did they get past me? But they were not like other men. They had this glow about them. One sat at the head and the other at the foot of where Jesus' body had been. When they spoke, their voices were like voices I have never heard. They said, "Woman, why are you crying?" To which I replied, "They have taken my Lord away, and I don't know where they have put him." (John 20:13). When I turned, the gardener was present; and he asked, "Woman why are you crying? Who is it you are looking for?" I pleaded with him to tell me where they had taken the Lord. Then he called my name, "Mary." Right at that moment, I realized that it was not the gardener at all—it was my Rabboni. It was Jesus! I reached out to touch him, but he replied, "Do not hold on to me, for I have not yet returned to the Father. Go instead to my brothers and tell them, 'I am returning to my Father and your Father, to my God and your God.'" (John 20:15–17). I bolted out of the garden and ran as fast as I could to tell the good news! As I ran, I knew that all the angry voices were gone—it was now *my voice* in my head, shouting with joy and proclaiming, "I have seen the Lord! I have seen the Lord!"

## The Lessons

I was transformed from a demon-possessed woman to a devoted disciple of Christ. Some have even called me the "apostle to the apostles."[10] I take no credit for anything. All the glory belongs to God. No matter what your plight in life is, once you meet Jesus Christ you will never be the same. Whatever you are, be it a wild, demon-possessed woman like I was, a harlot, an adulteress, a thief, or even a murderer, you too, can be transformed from your former condition to a fully devoted, usable, Disciple of the Lord Jesus Christ. Even if you are haunted by lingering memories of your sinful past, you must remember, the former is no more. You were dead in your transgressions and sins, but you are now alive again in Christ (Ephesians 2:1–5). Your past is nothing to be ashamed of—it is a testimony to the great power of Jesus Christ. I am the Mary whom seven demons was cast out. I struggled with periodic bouts of insanity. People will always remember me as the woman who was possessed and tormented by demons. But that is all in the past. The old Mary Magdalene died on the day she met Jesus. I am a new creation in Christ. The Scriptures teach us that, if anyone is in Christ, he is a new creation; the old has gone, the new has come.

Women have a prominent place in the Lord's life and ministry. We no longer are subservient creatures considered useless and good for only housekeeping and childbearing. Jesus ushered in a new era of respect and honor for women. He demonstrated to the world that women are significant. We are equal to men in essence, spirit, and soul. Jesus used women, to model before men, the importance and strength of women in sharing the good news of the Gospel of Jesus Christ. Jesus trampled over the walls of low self-worth and self-abasement. There is no reason for any woman to remain stuck with hopelessness and feelings of defeat, or even wallow in self-pity. All of our sins and diseases were nailed to the cross. "For by grace you have been saved, through faith, it is the gift of God, not by works, so that no one can boast." (Ephesians 2:8–9). Receive your healing with a heart of gratitude, and choose to follow Christ with everything that is in you.

There comes a time in life when every believer must decide what to do with the precious gift of salvation. How now shall you live? What is our response to the sacrificial gift God gave, when he sent Jesus to die for our sins? All who call him Lord owe him a debt that we cannot pay. Jesus paid the ultimate penalty that brought us from death to life. Here are the lessons from my life that you must embrace.

## A Devotion to Serving

The first lesson is to devote your life to serving the Lord. After the Lord cast out the seven demons, I could have returned to Magdala and lived a life of ease. I certainly had the means to do so. Nevertheless, when Jesus healed me from demonic possession, my heart was also changed. I was filled with so much gratitude that I wanted to linger. My soul hungered for more of his words, and more of his presence in my life. His truth was so powerful. So I turned away from Magdala to follow him. It was the best decision that I have ever made. What do you need to turn away from in order to devote your life to serving Jesus Christ?

I gave my life in service to Jesus, not fully understanding the price he would ultimately pay for my sins and yours. The Lord taught us to believe in something much greater than ourselves—ministry! Meeting needs. We walked the dusty roads and listened to his words. We helped the infirmed and ministered to the poor people in the towns and cities where the Lord traveled. I never wavered in my commitment to serving Jesus or his disciples. Jesus said, "I have come that they may have life, and have it to the full." (John 10:10). A full life is a life full of service. Why not enjoy the fullness of life by devoting your life to serving God and his people.

## A Devotion to Sharing

The second lesson is to devote your life to sharing. Ministry is costly, and you must count the costs if you desire to follow Christ. As a follower of Jesus Christ, I opened up my treasures to support the ministry. The women were among many of the disciples who provided for the Lord out of our own means (Luke 8:3). How can one benefit from so great of a gift, and not give in return? I had the financial means to share. My gratitude compelled me to give, so that others could benefit from the same healing that God had so graciously bestowed upon me. Many women temporarily left their homes to travel with Jesus and the disciples. Among us was Salome. Her husband owned a fishing business. She used some of those resources to support the ministry. Joanna, the wife of Cuza, who managed Herod's household, and Susanna was with us. They were holy women of God. We all served and used our resources to support the ministry (Luke 8:1–3). Even if you do not have the financial means, you have spiritual gifts that can be used in support of the ministry. Jesus liberated women from lowly positions to partners with him in ministry. Freely you have received—freely give (Matthew 10:7–8).

Finally, what made the church so powerful in its beginning was the liberality of the believers. The Scriptures teach us that, "All the believers were together and they had everything thing in common" (Acts 2:44). The believers sold their possessions and goods and gave to anyone that had a need (Acts 2:42). This attitude was attractive to the nonbelievers, and the Lord added thousands to the church. We all must be willing to share. Remember, God owns everything. The more we give, the more enriched our lives will be.

## A Devotion to Supporting

I have one final lesson to share with you and that is, my devotion to supporting. The more time I spent with Jesus, the more convinced I was that he was the Messiah. There was nothing to dissuade me otherwise. I had witnessed so many miracles; even I was the product of one such miracle. No man could speak with the power and authority that Jesus possessed—unless God had sent him. But not all of the disciples felt that way. There were truths spoken by Jesus that some could not accept; some of the disciples forsook Jesus and followed him no more (John 6:53–60). Many people will be offended by the truth, and there will be a great falling away. Nevertheless, we must be willing to become true followers of Jesus Christ, and not spectators and volunteers.

Remember, when the doubters begin to leave, these are the moments when our pastors and leaders need our support. As the truth becomes more evident, the journey gets lonelier. The crowds will begin to dwindle. Nevertheless, we must never waver in our support of the ministry. I never left the Lord's side, even when persecution and death were imminent. I wanted Jesus to know that I was there—still available to minister to his needs. I wanted him to see my face when the pain of the lashings became unbearable. I felt that somehow my support would give him the strength to keep going. You must do the same for the pastors and servant leaders that God has given charge over you.

A great price was paid for your sins and mine. Therefore, you must never waiver in your devotion to serving God. You must do your best to support the ministry financially. Give until it hurts. God will always supply you with more to give. Show up! Be present!

Support the work and the mission. It is our reasonable duty for the awesome sacrifice paid for our salvation.

Finally, I am telling my story so that you will have the assurance that Jesus Christ has the power to deliver you from any malady, including demonic possession. What this means for you is that you must tell your story of deliverance. Share your testimony with others. Go out and tell everyone exactly how Satan tried to destroy you, but failed!

## Study Questions

1. Who is Mary Magdalene and where did she come from?
2. What was Mary Magdalene's greatest struggle?
3. In what ways can demons influence Christians?
4. What did Mary Magdalene do after Jesus healed her from the seven demons?
5. What lessons does Mary Magdalene and the other women teach us about fellowship and service?
6. What lessons does this study teach us about how we should respond to people with spiritual strongholds such as, addictions, mental illnesses, and other physical ailments?
7. What caused many of the disciples to forsake Jesus? (John 6).
8. How did Jesus respond to the women in ancient times and what role did they play in his ministry?
9. What honor did Mary Magdalene receive because of her faithfulness and devotion to Jesus Christ? (John 20:16–17).

# 4

## Behind Door Four
## Tamar: A Defiled Princess in Isolation

> But she answered him, "No, my brother, do not force me, for no such thing should be done in Israel. Do not do this disgraceful thing!"
>
> 2 Samuel 13:12 NKJV

The room was spinning! Amnon was all over me. I pushed him as hard as I could and yelled, "Stop . . . get off me! Let me go. . . . Please stop!" Amnon's face was angry and contorted like an evil beast. A monster! My arms were pinned in an awkward position. I tried to move, but I could not. "No! No! No! Please!" I screamed. Then Amnon cupped my mouth with his hand. I tried to bite him but he pressed me so hard he nearly drove my head through the bed. "No, my brother, please stop!" I cried. My mouth was open—I was screaming—but I heard no sound. I was fighting as hard as I could. But Amnon overpowered me. He trashed me about like a rag doll. He was turning me, pinning me, pressing me—and squeezing me so tightly it hurt. He tried to kiss me, but I kept turning my head. I cried out again, "Stop! . . . Please my brother—please stop!"

My face was drenched with tears and sweat. My hair was everywhere—across my face—on Amnon's chest. By then, from the scuffle, my robe was wrapped so tightly around me I could barely move. Weakened from the struggle I pleaded desperately, "Please! Oh, please Amnon . . . my brother . . . do not force me." For a brief moment, he looked at me—his eyes welled up with tears. I thought he would stop—but he lay on top of me—and he raped me. There was blood! I could taste it in my mouth. I had bit my lip so hard that it bled. Then, the unthinkable happened. With the most intense hatred I had ever seen, Amnon yelled at me and said, "Get up and get out!" I yelled back at him, "No! Sending me away would be a greater wrong than what you have already done to me." Against all of my pleas, Amnon refused. He called in his personal servant and commanded him to throw me out and bolt the door behind me. Two unwelcomed men put their hands on me that day! All that I am, and all that I was to become, was brutally stripped away from me that day in Amnon's apartment. I was as good as dead. But it was not over! I am Tamar, and this is my story.

## When the Kings Ruled

It was during the time when Israel rejected God and desired a king to rule over them. Israel wanted to be governed like the heathen nations. God granted Israel's request and anointed Saul as Israel's first king. My father, David, was the second king to rule Israel. At the time, Israel did not understand the enormous perils involved when sinful men ruled nations. For example, kings often married pagan women to form political alliances, increase their fortunes, and strengthen their military might. Thus, polygamy increasingly became a common part of the culture in ancient Israel, especially for political reasons. These practices often lead Israel into idolatry and away from serving the only true God. My father also married foreign women. He had many concubines. Unsurprisingly, the integrity and structure of family life in ancient Israel began to erode with the practice of polygamy and idolatry.

My father was involved in many wars against the enemies of Israel. He formed political alliances with foreigners, who caused him to neglect his duties as a father. The mixed races, cultures, and religious practices among the wives and concubines, produced strong rivalries and dysfunction within the families. I believe that much of the trouble in the palace began with the erosion of the family structure.[1]

Amnon was my father's firstborn son. His mother, Ahinoam, was a Jezreelite. My brother Absalom and I were the children of my father's wife, Maacah. Maacah is the daughter of Talmai, the king of Gesher.[2] My father had eight wives and several concubines and children. One can only imagine what it was like to grow up in a palace with so many wives, concubines, and children. Multiple marriages are havens for dysfunction in families. My family was no different; for God never intended for man to engage in the practice of polygamy because polygamy creates an enormous hardship on the family. The women are especially degraded. They must submit themselves to a life in a much lower status than that of wives

## The Diabolical Plan

My father may have been neglectful as a parent because of all of his responsibilities, but he adored his children. So, when Amnon lay in his bed—pretending to be ill—my father came to visit him. By this time, Amnon had already conspired with his cousin, Jonadab, to devise a scheme to set a trap for me. The plan was to trick me into being alone with Amnon in his bedchamber. Sadly, they used my father to aid in their despicable conspiracy, of course without his knowledge.

Amnon was sick but not in any physical way. Amnon believed that he was in love with me—but his love was twisted and perverted. Our laws forbade sexual immorality, and incest was punishable by death. Amnon knew that it was forbidden by law for him to marry his sister and that our father would never permit such a marriage (Leviticus 18:6–22). Incest and other deviant sexual relations were the practices of pagans and heathen nations, like the Egyptians and the Canaanites. It was common for Egyptian kings to marry their sisters to maintain kingdom rulership. They believed that incest preserved the purity of the royal bloodline and that only the king's descendants were entitled to rule in Egypt. But it was not so from the beginning in ancient Israel.[3] The Mosaic Law strictly forbade us to approach anyone who is near of kin or to uncover his or her nakedness (Leviticus 18:6). My brother Amnon knew that it was an abomination to practice such wickedness in Israel. So he made himself sick, because he lusted after what he knew was unlawful for him to have. There were practices among the Patriarchs, whereby marriages were permissible among near kin, such as in the case of our Father Abraham's marriage to Sarah (Genesis 20:12). Nevertheless, Amnon's scheme went against the spirit of the Mosaic Law.

When Amnon's cousin and confidant Jonadab noticed his frail appearance, he pressed him to tell him what was in his heart (2 Samuel 13:4). After Amnon told Jonadab that he was in love with me, Jonadab exploited Amnon's weakness and devised an evil plan to trap me. Jonadab was a crafty and wicked man. He was never truly Amnon's friend. Jonadab never had Amnon's best interests at heart. Rather than warn him of the deviant and unnatural nature of his feelings toward his sister, and even the outcome if he acted on those feelings, Jonadab devised the vilest and most wicked plan to bring evil against King David's household. His plan was designed to hurt rather than help Amnon. Jonadab did not know that, "A friend loves at all times." (Proverbs 17:17). True friendship is based on mutual love and respect, which is a quality of the relationship that was never possessed by neither Amnon nor Jonadab.

## My Torn Ornamental Robe

I thought it was odd when my father requested that I go to Amnon's house and prepare food for him. Amnon had the best servants available to prepare food for him. Not only did he have servants in his house, he had the privilege of eating the finest foods directly from the kings table. Nevertheless, I honored my father's request and went to my brother's house to bake him bread.

I wore my ornamental robe that day—a garment that represented my purity and royal status as a princess (2 Samuel 13:18). I thought nothing about baking the cakes for Amnon in his presence. After all, he was my brother and I had no reason to be concerned about being alone with him in his chamber. But when Amnon refused to eat the bread that I sat before him, I felt uneasy. I became even more suspicious when he dismissed the servants and requested that I bring the cakes into the bedroom so that he could eat from my hand. In my culture, unmarried women are forbidden to be in the company of a man alone. Since Amnon was my brother, I naively thought that I would be safe with him. I was wrong. When I brought the cakes to his bed as he requested, Amnon grabbed me and said, "Come lie with me, my sister" (2 Samuel 13:10). When I refused, he forced me! I pleaded with Amnon not to do such an abominable act. Incest is a terrible crime that brings shame upon not only the victim and the family, but also the whole nation. Deviant sexual practices of any kind were against God's law. We are God's chosen people and as God is holy, so he has called us to holiness (1 Peter 1:16). That is the reason the penalties for breaking such laws were severe, including death.

The laws governing rape in my culture did not favor women. If a man was found guilty of rape he was to be stoned to death (Deuteronomy 22:23–27). Nevertheless, if a woman did not protest or cry out loudly enough, she could be blamed for the rape and even stoned to death. She is now considered defiled, even if the rape was deemed no fault of her own. Women victimized by rape have always had to defend themselves vigorously. Rather than the rapist being on trial, the victim is—and has to prove that she is innocent of any lewd behavior that may have enticed the rapist. In some cases, she must prove that the rape actually happened. Not much has changed over the centuries.

My shame was unbearable. There was no turning back once Amnon trapped and raped me. I was forever marred by the stench and shame of what he had done to me. I closed my eyes and hoped with everything in me that this was only a bad dream. But I was startled back to reality by Amnon's hateful and angry outburst. He said, "Get up and get out." I yelled back at him, "No! Sending me away would be a greater wrong than what you have already done to me!" (2 Samuel 13:15–16). I tried to hold on to him, but he pulled away. Amnon's eyes were filled with rage and contempt when he called for the servant and said, "Get this woman out of here and bolt the door after her!" (2 Samuel 13:17). The servant grabbed me and threw me out! My knees scraped hard on the stone floor. When I landed, a part of the hem of my robe was caught in the door. I was shaken when I heard the latch on the door slide into place. I cannot say how long I sat there— crying and trying to put things into perspective. I could barely breathe. I coughed as I choked on my tears. Then, in anguish, I cried out with a loud voice and tore my robe. I grabbed ashes and placed them on my head. As I stood, I yanked my robe from the door and cried out again as loudly as I could. My voice was so loud I could hear the echo of my cries bouncing off the palace walls. I sobbed and ran as fast as I could. Through my tears, I could see images of people as I passed them. I fell down again! Someone placed a hand on my shoulder to comfort me, but I pulled away, stood to my feet, and continued to run. I placed my hand on my head and ran as fast as I could run. I ran . . . I just ran as fast as I could!

## The Murderous Plot

When my brother Absalom saw me, he asked, "Has that Amnon, your brother, been with you? Be quiet now, my sister; he is your brother, don't take this thing to heart." (2 Samuel 13:20). "Be quiet! Don't take it to heart!" But, I had already taken every moment of that dreadful day to heart! "How can I be silent when something so filthy—so violent—and so vile has just happened to me! Is there no comfort for me? Is there no justice for the wrong that has been done to me?" From that day forward, Absalom, my beloved brother, took me to his house.

In the days that followed my father heard about all that Amnon did to me, but he said nothing. He was angry, but he went on being king and never punished Amnon for raping me. Absalom took care of me, and when he spoke to Amnon, he said neither good nor bad to him (2 Samuel 13:22). Absalom knew that Amnon was a wicked man. In all probability, this was not the first time that Amnon had raped or violated an innocent woman. Unfortunately, as in times past, he got away with it.

I knew my brother Absalom hated Amnon with a deep passion! Absalom was biding his time to take action, but I had no idea what he planned; he kept these things hidden in his heart. For two years, I suffered in silence. I had nightmares. I was haunted by flashes and visions of Amnon's face and the violent attack against me. At times, even Amnon's words rang out in my mind. I was frightened most of the time—especially at night. I carefully watched every man that came near me. Whenever I heard a loud noise of any kind, I would nearly jump out of my skin. For days on end, I agonized over what I had lost the day my brother Amnon raped me. I was so miserable and lonely. I had hoped to be married one day, perhaps become a queen. I wanted a family and children of my own. But all of that was shattered when my virginity was wasted on a crime of passion! Then, the unthinkable happened.

It was sheepshearing time so my brother Absalom gathered his sheepshearers at Baal Hazor. Baal Hazor was in a remote area near the border of Ephraim.[4] For two years, Absalom nursed his hatred toward Amnon and waited for an opportune time to carry out revenge. He plotted to kill Amnon for what he did to me. Some also believe that Absalom wanted to kill Amnon so that he would be next in line for the throne. Somehow, Absalom convinced the king to allow all of his brothers, including Amnon, to attend the feast to celebrate with him at Baal Hazor. It is no wonder that my father granted Absalom's request. Perhaps he felt this gesture would somehow bring the brothers closer together. After all, sheepshearing time was a festive time of drunkenness, revelry, and in some instances, settling old scores.[5] Unbeknown to everyone, Absalom had instructed his servants to wait until Amnon was merry with wine and kill him. And they did. Absalom used his servants to murder his older brother, Amnon.

It was a terrible night! When Amnon was murdered, everyone scattered and rushed back to the palace. When my father received the news, he tore his robe and fell to the ground. There was wailing, mourning, and grieving so great, it was heard throughout the palace. Even I felt sorrow for Amnon. Now, I would lose two brothers—for it was unlawful for anyone to take vengeance in his own hands, even to right the wrong done to me. There was no excuse for Absalom to avenge my rape by killing Amnon. Now, there was no turning back for Absalom. He had no place to run. He had committed a crime punishable by death, so he could not go to the cities of refuge (Numbers 35:9–15). Absalom could not return to the kingdom or to his home. So, he fled to our mother's home in Geshur. There, he could live under the protective hand of our grandfather, Talmai, the King of Geshur. Absalom spent three years in exile in Geshur—and I was alone . . . again.

## My Father's Failure

My father was a great warrior and Israel's beloved king. With all of his failures and faults and even his sins, he was still a man after God's own heart. King David was a sweet psalmist. Whatever one might think of my father, he demonstrated to all of us the joys and victories in serving the only true and living God. Through his failures, we were able to see the graciousness and mercy of Almighty God. He wrote many Psalms and confessed openly his faults. He taught us how to unashamedly, worship God, and the importance of humbling ourselves before God in repentance when we sinned. Unfortunately, these lessons were not cemented in all of our hearts. My father was guilty of many things: adultery, murder, polygamy, disobedience, and he failed to take charge of his children. Still, he was God's anointed king—the ruddy shepherd boy that God raised from the sheepfold to the palace. He slew the mighty Philistine giant, Goliath, and killed tens of thousands of the Lord's enemies! He played the sweet music on the harp that brought comfort to a king tortured by demons. Yes, King David was the greatest king to rule in Israel. But, he had many weaknesses, just like you and me.

My father did not come to my bedside when he heard that Amnon had raped me. He did not come to hold me and comfort me at a time when I desperately needed reassurance. King David never told me that I was still a precious jewel in his crown, regardless of the assault on my body. He did not dry my tears or kiss away my sorrow—as a father should. What is worst of all, he did not punish Amnon for the evil that he had done to me, nor did he apologize for not protecting me. After all, my father sent me to Amnon's house in the first place. He visited Amnon's bedside when he was sick—why not me? I waited and I waited.

In the days that followed, I longed for my father. But he never came. Only Absalom was there. How many assaults can one take? What am I to believe about my worth and myself in the sight of my father? Was I now so repulsive that he could not look upon me? I was viewed as a fornicator in the eyes of my people—I was defiled and unfit for marriage.[6] What about my father? How do I respond to my father's negligence? It seemed that he protected Amnon more than he protected me. Perhaps if he had punished Amnon, things would have been different. Maybe my brother Absalom would not have taken matters into his own hands. My father's response to the rape was an even greater assault. His silence and inattention drove me deeper into isolation. Nevertheless, he was my father and I loved him—so I forgave him.

## The Lessons

A rapist is not always a shadowy figure lurking behind bushes, prowling in a dark alley or wearing a trench coat and hiding out in some vacant lot or building. A rapist can be anyone—male or female. A rapist can be an acquaintance or a stranger, a prince or a pauper. A rapist can be a priest, schoolteacher, father, uncle, friend or even the man sitting next to you in a church, or the synagogue.

When a woman is raped, she may not show visible signs of the rape on the outside, but she is changed forever on the inside. She never truly feels safe again. She is watchful and more keenly sensitive to her surroundings. The recurrent dreams and intrusive images of her rape may never go away. She often replays the events in her mind, and questions even her actions—*could she have prevented it somehow?* She may blame herself for what happened to her. However, nothing could be further from the truth. That is a lie from the pit of hell! You are not at fault, and you are not alone.

## Rape is Not the Victim's Fault

The first lesson is that rape is not the victims fault. No matter what the rapist says, rape is never about love or anything that the victim has done. Rape is one of the vilest and most degrading acts that one can commit against another human being. It is a detestable and hateful assault against another person. Rape has nothing to do with seduction on the part of the victim. Unfortunately, as in my culture, societies tend to blame the victim more than the offender. Sometimes, the rapist receives more protection under the law than the victim does.

The effects of rape can be devastating to the victim, and depending on the nature of the crime, some victims never recover fully. In some cases, rape can be violent and cause permanent injury or even death. Many victims of rape are haunted by vivid memories, dreams or other reenactments of the rape itself. In ancient Israel, we were not immune to sexually transmitted diseases. Unfortunately, the emotional scars can be more damaging than the rape itself. Thus, it is important for victims of rape, not to blame themselves or allow themselves to embrace self-condemnation, self-doubt, fear, guilt, and even reject the reality that you are still "Fearfully and wonderfully made" (Psalm 139:14).

## Rape is Not an Act of Love

The second lesson is, rape is not an expression of love. Rape is an act of control. My brother Amnon thought that he loved me. However, in truth, Amnon saw me as nothing more than an object to be desired. He was attracted to my beauty and my virtue. He lusted after my body so intensely that it made him sick. Love had nothing to do with Amnon's actions against me. Love and lust mixes like oil and water. Love does not make one sick to the point of not being able to eat nor does it pine away over that which is forbidden.

Love is patient and kind (1 Corinthians 13). Love honors and waits. Love never forces itself on another person nor is love intrusive, threatening, or harmful. Love never takes, robs or steals someone's dignity—it never humiliates or victimizes another person for one's own self-gratification. Rape is never about expressing feelings of love. Rape is a cunning, sexually aggressive behavior that seeks its own pleasure—rather than the respect, honor, and well-being of another person.

Finally, love is not cunning or calculating. Love thinks no evil; love protects and avoids causing harm at all costs. Love believes all things, hopes all things, and endures all things (1 Corinthians

13:5–7). Love is the greatest gift that God has given us. There was nothing lovely or loving about my brother's actions toward me.

## Tell Your Story

The final lesson is probably the most difficult of all. You must tell your story. Countless women live in fear and isolation because of the shame and indignity of rape. Many never report that they have been raped because of the stigma attached to rape—the disgrace of the crime itself—feelings of guilt, and the person's distress over the way they will be viewed by family, friends, and society as a whole.

My brother Absalom, in his misguided effort to protect me from further harm said, "But now, hold your peace, my sister. He is your brother; do not take this thing to heart" (2 Samuel 13:20). Unfortunately, Absalom did not understand the painful emotional struggles, that I now, and would later endure from this devastating assault on my body. He did not understand what it meant to be degraded in this way. My soul cried out to be heard! I wanted to be vindicated, but I kept silent. All of the anguish, grief, torment, and pain I felt were wrapped tightly in a knot in my stomach—crying out to be released! Sill I kept silent. However, you must not.

It is important for you to release all of your emotions. Let go of the shame, regret, hurt, self-blame, and sorrow. Report it! Tell what happened to a caring and loving friend, counselor, or clergywoman. Tell what happened to someone who will come along side you in prayer and help you through your pain. Your suffering is not for naught. It is through trials and testing that we accomplish God's will for our lives—no matter how bitter the experience is. The Lord is able to wipe away every tear and restore all that has been destroyed in your life. Your earthly father may not be there for you, but your Heavenly Father is always near (Psalm 34:17–18).

Finally, out of this tragic event came the most marvelous gift—God's grace and comfort. I found a place of solace in the arms of God's glorious grace. He comforted me and gave me a new perspective. Remember, not everything that happens to us will be good. We will experience evil too. Job said it this way: "Shall we indeed accept good from God, and not trouble." (Job 2:10). Rather than focus on the tragedy, why not focus on the power of Almighty God to restore what you have lost. God is able to heal you and make you whole again. Jesus said, "In the world you will have trouble. But take heart! I have overcome the world." (John 16:33). No matter what happens to you, good or bad, remember the Lord is with you and if you rest in him, you will have peace.

The days following my rape were difficult. I had to cope with the shame, overcome the guilt and self-blame, and learn to live with what I had lost. The one constant in my life was the presence of Almighty God. I have learned to focus on what is good, righteous, and pure in my life. I have learned to train my brain to think on these things; what is true, noble, just, pure and lovely, highly regarded, virtuous and praiseworthy. (Philippians 4:8). God's love is what makes my life valuable. That is why I chose to live in the present rather than the past. No, my father was not present in the aftermath of the rape, but my God never left me! Therefore, in my greatest hour of despair, I rested in him. I found peace because the arms of grace held me and reassured me that all was well!

You have a choice. You can rest in God and ask him to help you make sense of the tragic events of your life or you can wallow in self-pity and allow yourself to be a victim who never recovers.

My earthly father failed me, but my Heavenly Father restored all that was lost—both physically and emotionally—by granting me a new spiritual perspective. If you call His name, it will not be in vain. In the words of my father King David, "Cast your cares on the Lord and he will sustain you; he will never let the righteous fall." (Psalm 55:22).

*The Struggles of Unloved Women*

# Study Questions

1. What was Tamar wearing when she entered Amnon's house? What was the significance of her attire?
2. Why did kings marry multiple wives in ancient Israel?
3. How did polygamy affect King David's household?
4. What kind of father was David toward his children?
5. What kind of friend was Jonadab to Amnon?
6. How did Amnon feel about Tamar? Why do you think he raped her?
7. Why do you think Absalom immediately suspected that Amnon had raped Tamar?
8. What was King David's response to Tamar's the rape?
9. In Ancient Israel, rape and incest were severely punished. Why do you think David did not punish Amnon for raping Tamar? (Leviticus18:9; 20:17).
10. In what ways are modern societal views about rape similar to ancient Israel's views?
11. What role does forgiveness have in Tamar's tragic story? How should we respond to our parents when they fall short, as in the case of King David?

## Behind Door Five
### Hannah: A Prayer and a Vow Fulfilled

"No my lord, I am a woman of sorrowful spirit. I have drunk neither wine nor intoxicating drink, but have poured out my soul before the Lord."

1 Samuel 1:15

It was not a good day. As was our yearly practice, we traveled to Shiloh to worship the Lord at the temple. Peninnah was in rare form that day. At every opportunity, she made it a point to remind me of my barrenness. She paraded her children before me and mocked me with sarcasm and insensitive comments. She rolled her eyes at me and sneered at me from across the table—especially when Elkanah was not paying attention. It was childish and pathetic—I was sick of it! By the time we sat down to eat, I had had my fill of Elkanah, Peninnah, and her noisy, chattering, children! What's more, my heart was filled with sorrow—much more than at other times. I was depressed and desperate. I lamented over my childlessness, "Am I cursed?" It was difficult to hold back my tears. I felt like I would explode. I wanted to run out of the room as fast as I could. This has gone on too long—not only for me, but for Elkanah too. I could not eat of the peace offering because Peninnah had provoked me relentlessly that day. My heart was so heavy. I wanted to lash out at Peninnah, but I held my peace. It took every ounce of my strength to control my emotions. My head felt like it would split in half. Then, Elkanah looked at me and in an attempt to comfort me he said, "Hannah, why do you weep? Why do you not eat? And why is your heart grieved? Am I not better to you than ten sons?" (1 Samuel 1:8). Elkanah was kind and I knew what he was trying to do, but I could not find any comfort in his words. Nevertheless, he was right; he had been better to me than ten sons. So I ate and drank. Then I went to the temple to pray. I am Hannah, and this is my story.

## A Husband's Dilemma

Elkanah, whose name means, "God is Possessing" was a Levite—a descendant of the Kohathites, one of the honorable families of the priestly line of Jacob. Elkanah was a devout and godly man. He grew up in the hill country of Ephraim in a place called Ramathaim Zophim, which in the Hebrew language means "Double Height of the Watchers."[1] Ephraim was close to Jerusalem and Shiloh, the place where we made our annual trek to worship and offer sacrifices to the Lord.

Elkanah was an honorable man, but he practiced polygamy. Polygamy was a well-established practice in my culture. It was practiced mostly for political reasons and by wealthy families who could afford the cost of a bride. Polygamy enabled families to increase their wealth and social status. Many men practiced polygamy to have children, especially when their wives were barren. Polygamy created a great deal of hardship and contributed to the deterioration of families in ancient Israel. It was especially difficult for women because it caused bitterness, hostility, and conflict between the unfortunate women who lived in polygamous households. It is very difficult to maintain harmony in a home where a man's affections are divided between multiple women. In the Hebrew culture, the second wife was referred to as the "rival wife." Thus, Peninnah and I were constantly embroiled in unfriendliness and contention.

For me, polygamy was a constant reminder of the sin and moral corruption of my beloved nation. After all, God had chosen the Israelites to be his people, set apart to be a "peculiar treasure" above all nations (Exodus 19:5). The Israelites were assured of prominence and prosperity as God's chosen people, as long as we did not rebel against his Law. Unfortunately, as a nation, we fought many wars, and suffered many adversities because we disobeyed the Mosaic Law.

## My Barrenness and Vexation

Peninnah was no different from any other woman in a relationship where two women share the same man. In polygamous marriages, one wife is favored more than the other wife. Although she bore many children for Elkanah, Peninnah was never honored as I was. Elkanah's affections were always turned more in my direction. Peninnah struggled with this, so she became my adversary.

My longings for a child and Peninnah's taunts were a daily source of hostility and vexation. In my culture, barrenness was viewed as a curse from God and Peninnah used this as a weapon of scorn and reproach against me (1 Samuel 1:6). Children were considered a blessing from God. They were important to the extension of the family line. Children were also a source of security, especially in old age. When it was time to make an offering to the Lord, Elkanah would give each of us portions of the meat. Elkanah always gave me a double portion (1 Samuel 1:4–5). Peninnah struggled in a marriage of convenience. She knew that she was nothing more than a means for childbearing and that Elkanah's heart belonged to me. So she lashed out at me with jealous rants and taunts. She was vindictive. Her constant mocking and spitefulness was a thorn in my flesh. It was very difficult to live with her. There is nothing more unpleasant than being the victim of someone else's jealousy. Peninnah struggled with insecurity and she lacked confidence. She spent days on end finding ways to provoke me. Nevertheless, I held my peace.

## A Prayer and a Promise

We spent the day in Shiloh at the temple worshiping and offering sacrifices to God. At that time, Eli served as one of the last judges and the high priest of the tabernacle. He had two sons, Hophni and Phinehas, who were also serving as priests in the temple at Shiloh. Hophni and Phinehas were wicked. They did not know the Lord—yet they served as priests in the temple.

Hophni and Phinehas made the people despise the offering of the Lord. They did not consecrate themselves for their service in the temple. Instead, they forced the worshippers to give them the better of the offerings first by taking the raw meat before it was burned on the altar of the Lord. They caused the people to violate the Law of the Peace Offering, which mandated that the peace offering be boiled and eaten in the court of the tabernacle. What remained was burned with fire so that the Lord received the blood and the fat (Leviticus 7:31–32).[3] Hophni and Phinehas frustrated the people by restricting them from performing the sacrifice as it was written in the Law of Moses (Leviticus 7:29–32). The priests were always provided with ample portions of the offering. But Eli's sons were greedy, immoral, and wicked to the core. They did not reverence the holy things of God and threatened to take the offering by force if the people did not do as they commanded. Consequently, the worshippers were embittered when they went to the temple to offer sacrifices to the Lord.

Hophni and Phinehas sinned greatly before the Lord. Not only did they take advantage of the worshippers, but they also had sexual relations with the women who served in the temple (1 Samuel 2:23). Eli knew what his sons were doing, but he did nothing to protect the worshippers from being bullied, nor did he protect the women from being sexually abused.

As we sat to eat our portions of the sacrifice, Elkanah gave Peninnah and her children a share of meat, but he always gave me a double portion of the peace offering. Peninnah despised Elkanah's favor toward me. Her taunts that day were relentless, and I was grieved to the point of tears. I was so depressed I could not eat. Elkanah noticed that I did not eat my portion of the peace offering. He was frustrated by his attempts to console me, so he confronted me for not eating. His gentle reproof was not just out of concern for my appetite—for this was a feast of joy rather than mourning.[4] Elkanah was frustrated by my sadness. It seemed his actions toward me did little to reassure me of his love and devotion. After all, he *was* better to me than ten sons. But I spent my days and nights agonizing over my barrenness. I believed that God had closed my womb and there was nothing Elkanah or the taunts of Peninnah could do to change my condition. For his part, Elkanah did all he could to comfort me. He gave me a double portion of the sacrifice every year and he reassured me of my position as his first wife; he never wavered in his devotion to me. Although I felt secure of his love for me, I spent my time in the valley of sorrow, rather than focusing on the many blessings I had.

Then, out of frustration and exasperation, Elkanah reminded me that my attention was on the wrong thing. Why should I wallow in tears of sorrow and neglect my duty to God?[5] Why was I not grateful for the many blessings I already enjoyed? Every day was a day filled with new mercies and I had more than enough for which to be thankful. Even if God chose to close my womb forever, he was faithful and still my sovereign Lord. Sometimes we lose heart by focusing more on what we do not have rather than being grateful for what we do have. We waste precious time living in a pit of sorrow and grief, and miss the joy of the gift of life. Yes, I was childless. Nevertheless, I could have chosen to be "better than ten sons" to Elkanah. I had so much to be thankful for, regardless of Peninnah's constant provocations. Elkanah was a godly man, and I had his love and support, no matter what Peninnah did to provoke me. More than that, I had the amazing grace of God, which was far better than a house filled with children, or anything the world could offer. So I took heed to what Elkanah said, and I ate and drank.

When the meal ended, I went to the temple to pray. I bowed before the Lord and I cried out to him in bitterness of soul. I labored in prayer. I cried out to God and said, "Oh Lord Almighty, if you will only look upon your servant's misery and remember me, and not forget your servant, but give her a son, then I will give him to the Lord for all the days of his life, and no razor will ever be used on his head." (1 Samuel 1:11). No words could express my heart's petition. I prayed forcefully and fervently. I shut out everything around me and focused only on communing with God. Then, I was startled by the most objectionable accusation! Eli the priest, approached me and said, "How long will you keep on getting drunk? Get rid of your wine." (1 Samuel 1:14).

## My Vow and Vindication

I was not drunk! I feared the Lord—unlike Eli's wicked sons Hophni and Phinehas. How dare he accuse me! Eli's lack of compassion towards God's people was evident and typical of this undeserved accusation. He failed to control his sons—and they did not honor him as a father or as the high priest. Perhaps, he was too old and feeble to wrestle with his sons. Regardless of the reasons, Eli hurled a false accusation against me; so I respectfully and humbly told him all that was in my heart. I said, "Not so, my lord, I am a woman who is deeply troubled. I have not been drinking wine or beer; I was pouring out my soul to the Lord. Do not take your servant for a wicked woman; I have been praying here out of my great anguish and grief." (1 Samuel 1:15–16).

I have discovered that there is no need to fret when priests, ministers, or any servant of God fails to honor God's people or devote themselves to the things of God. Just pray. Regardless of Eli's accusations, I honored him as the high priest. Hophni and Phinehas were despicable priests and Eli failed to discipline them for threatening God's people and seducing the women. But God did not allow Eli's negligence to stand in the way of my petition. In the end, Eli encouraged me with a blessing. He said, "Go in peace, and may the God of Israel grant you what you have asked of him." (1 Samuel 1:17). I made a vow that day. I asked God to give me a male child. I promised God that if he would look on my affliction and not forget me, I would give my son back to the Lord to serve him all the days of his life (1 Samuel 1:11). The Lord lifted my burden. My grief was relieved and my countenance brightened. I left the temple and returned to Elkanah.

Before we made our way home, we woke up early the next morning and went back to the temple to worship the Lord. Elkanah comforted me that day, and in the course of time, God answered my prayer and blessed us with a son. I called him Samuel, "Because I asked the Lord for him" (1 Samuel 1:19).

## The Providence of Almighty God

Children are a gift from God. I did not know it at the time, but the providence of God was at work in my life. No matter how much I agonized over my barrenness, in God's own timing, he gave me Samuel. Not only that, the Lord prepared Elkanah for his perfect will to be accomplished in Samuel's life. In my culture, a husband had the right to cancel a vow made by his wife (Numbers 30:6–8). Elkanah never resisted my vow to give Samuel back to the Lord. Even in the midst of Peninnah's taunts, God was working out his plan for my life. For that reason, we must hold fast to God in times of struggle and not waste time torturing ourselves over what we do not have. For too long, I focused on my barrenness and failed to enjoy all the other blessings God had provided. I wasted so much time complaining and grieving. God was in the midst of my sorrow; but I was so distracted by my condition, that I could not hear his voice or feel his presence. Consequently, I missed many opportunities for service and worship and I failed to enjoy the gracious gift God had given me in my marriage to Elkanah.

Samuel was a beautiful child in appearance and temperament. Elkanah continued to make his annual trip to Shiloh to offer sacrifices to the Lord, but I stayed behind until Samuel was weaned. As soon as Samuel was weaned, I planned to traveled with Elkanah to Shiloh and leave Samuel with Eli the high priest—just as I vowed. You may be wondering how I could leave my son with Eli and his two wicked sons. Well, I made a vow to give my son back to the Lord all the days of his life. Sometimes out of desperation our mouths can cause us to sin. Promises made to God must never be taken lightly (Deuteronomy 23:21–23). I was distressed when I prayed for Samuel. However, one must never be foolish and make a vow that one cannot keep out of desperation (Ecclesiastes 5:5–6). I hurried to pay what I owed to the Lord and in doing so, I knew he would take care of his gift to me. I had no doubt that Samuel would thrive in the care of God rather than in the hands of Eli or Hophni and Phinehas.

## My Joyful Heart and Praise

After Samuel was weaned, I returned to Shiloh with Elkanah to bring our sacrifices to the tabernacle. When I saw Eli the priest, I reminded him of who I was and presented Samuel to him. I told Eli all that God had done and how I vowed to lend Samuel to the Lord all the days of his life. We worshiped the Lord and presented our sacrifice in fulfillment of our vow to give Samuel back to the Lord.

I rejoiced in the Lord that day. My soul was on fire as I prayed. I remembered how my sorrow had turned to joy. I praised the Lord for who he is. God resists the proud and exalts the lowly. He humbled my enemies and made me rejoice. I rejoiced in the Lord for every barren woman and every person of low degree. I praised God for lifting the lowly and raising the poor. God takes the beggar from a heap of ashes, sets them among princes, and makes them inherit the throne of glory! I worshiped God for being Ruler and Owner of all things. He is our Creator—everything belongs to him. God keeps his saints and casts the wicked into darkness. He will judge the ends of the earth (1 Samuel 2:1–10).

Some women are highly skilled at fighting with their tongues. Peninnah was. Out of the depths of her pain, she provoked me with insults, hateful taunts, and contemptuous criticisms. For me, it was unbearable at times. Still, I did not have the heart to be at war with her, especially over something that I could not change. Too often, we fight against each other, but our enemy is unseen. The battle is against spiritual forces of evil in the heavenly realms. For we wrestle not against flesh and blood (Ephesians 6:12). An enemy within all of us wars against the Spirit. Peninnah was never my enemy. She made herself an enemy of God and he silenced her by blessing my womb. Through all of my struggles, I learned many lessons. God is sovereign. The Lord is the God of knowledge, and by him, actions are weighed. (2 Samuel 3b). He will bless whom he will bless and curse whom he will curse. Remember, we are in control our wills. It was my choice to agonize over my barrenness. I chose unwisely. It was Peninnah's choice to vex me. She too chose unwisely. However, in the end, God was glorified and I am graciously blessed to tell my story.

## The Lessons

Many women are childless. Some may struggle with barrenness for years. Nevertheless, if it is God's will, in the course of time, he will open their barren wombs. Still, others may never have the blessed privilege of giving birth to children. In either case, God is still our glorious heavenly Father. He is all knowledge. From the foundations of the earth, he knew and knows every detail of your life. Whatever he has ordained for your life will happen. However, no matter how strong or how spiritual you are, there will be times when your knees will buckle under the pressures of life, and the stress of your childlessness will cause great sorrow. Give yourself permission to mourn your barrenness, but do not mourn as if you have no hope. Even if God chooses to close your womb forever, he still has a wonderful plan for your life. These are the lessons I would like to share with you.

# Become a Woman of Prayer

There is nothing more sacred and powerful than prayer. The Lord bids us to "Come to me, all you who labor and are heavy laden, and I will give you rest." (Matthew 11:28). God invites us to come to him when we have burdens that seem unbearable. Barrenness is a burden that you cannot bear without God's comfort and reassurance that everything will work out for your good in the end. God encourages us to cast our cares upon him—for he cares for us (1 Peter 5:7). God wants us to acknowledge our weaknesses, humble ourselves, and submit to him. He will take care of our concerns. God does not want us to walk alone, especially in our trials. He is always there waiting for us to kneel before him and humbly bow in prayer.

Nothing catches God by surprise. He knows our struggles. Whatever the circumstances might be, whether barrenness, loss of a loved one, a challenging or abusive relationship, an addiction, an unloving husband, a disobedient child—perhaps you have been betrayed or taken advantage of—whatever your concerns are, God is waiting for you. There is power even in the most timid prayer.

Prayer is the heartbeat of every believer's life. Through prayer, we communicate to God our praise and worship, our concerns, and our deepest desires. Prayer enables us to fulfill our calling. Through prayer, we are able to influence the world in powerful ways. When we pray, we find strength and direction when we are lost, hope when we despair, and answers to our most perplexing dilemmas.

Finally, there are some things that can only be accomplished through prayer and fasting (Matthew 17:21). We must pray without ceasing; and we must pray persistently and fervently for one another.

The Lord prayed during his struggles and throughout his ministry. He won the victory in Gethsemane and overcame the shame of Calvary because he persisted in his prayers to our Father. Thus, we too must practice the spiritual discipline of prayer.

## Become a Woman of Grace

In the Hebrew language, *Hannah* means "gracious" or "graciousness." Grace is an expression of God's character; the Lord is full of grace and truth (John 1:14). Grace is a spiritual quality, which enables us to be agreeable and acceptable toward others. Grace moves us to give to someone what he or she does not deserve. Peninnah was in need of compassion—she was not my enemy, so I did not repay her evil taunts with evil retorts. Instead, I held my peace. For the battle was not mine it belonged to the Lord (1 Samuel 17:47).

Whenever someone wages war against you, it is a battle against the Lord. Peninnah was not fighting me; she was battling personal struggles by lashing *out* at me. Even if we have to suffer for righteousness' sake, we are blessed (1 Peter 3:14). It is not God's will for us to repay evil for evil; for what would that profit us? No one wins in a carnal fight (2 Corinthians 10:4). Our weapons are spiritual and we are to defeat error with the truth of God's Word.[6]

Finally, keep your tongue from evil. Refrain from returning insults with insults, instead, "Sanctify the Lord God in your hearts, and always be ready to give a defense to everyone who asks you a reason for the hope that is in you, with meekness and fear." (1 Peter 3:15). Perhaps, you will suffer for doing right. However, never allow pride to direct your conduct, especially toward people who revile you. Instead, give a soft answer, because a meek and quiet spirit is very precious to the Lord (1Peter 3:4). My response to Peninnah was peaceful rather than quarrelsome; and my home was the better for it.

## Become a Godly Mother

Regardless of the circumstances of the birth of our children, whether in a monogamous marriage, a polygamous marriage, or even outside of marriage, children are a gift from God (Psalm 127:3). One of the highest honors for a woman is to be a godly mother and to raise godly children. Every child needs nurturing, love, and godly influence. The time I spent weaning Samuel was precious. I taught him to worship the Lord, nurtured him, and prepared him for what was ahead. I prepared him to be separated from me and to serve God, even in the midst of evil and wantonness. Motherhood is not just about having a child to meet the demands of culture or for social acceptance. Being a mother is a privilege—for not all women can have children. Motherhood brings joy and sorrow, pleasure and bitterness. Nevertheless, we are called to be godly role models, teachers, and nurturers for our children.

I let go of that which was most precious to me and honored my vow. In turn, God called Samuel as one of his most faithful and honored priests. It was a time when Israel needed godly leadership in the temple. Samuel was called by God before he was conceived. I was the vessel God used to bring Samuel into his priestly ministry. It was the providential will of God. We have no earthly idea who our children will become. That is why it is necessary for women to be godly mothers and role models. I made Samuel a little robe and brought it with me when we came up to offer our yearly sacrifices

(1 Samuel 2:19). By God's grace, Samuel grew into one of Israel's most beloved and revered priests.

Finally, many mothers have given their children to God for the sake of the Kingdom. Mary, the mother of Jesus, was a godly mother. She rejoiced in the day that God showed her favor and blessed her womb with our Lord and Savior Jesus Christ (Luke 1:46–55). However, her joy turned to much sorrow as she watched her son suffer for us. The prophet Isaiah wrote, "But he was pierced for our transgressions, he was crushed for our iniquities; the punishment that brought us peace was upon him, and by his wounds we are healed." (Isaiah 53:5). The stripes Jesus took brought salvation to all of us. Mary grieved, but when Jesus was raised from the dead, joy came—and deliverance came for all of us! For all the mothers who raise godly children and put their trust in Jesus Christ, no matter what happens, joy will come! What more can I say; neither time, nor space in my life's story will permit me to tell you all the reasons for you to be a godly mother. Embrace the lessons.

## Study Questions

1. Elkanah was a devout and godly man. In what ways did the culture influence his behavior?
2. Hannah's name means "grace" or "graciousness." How did her character reflect the meaning of her name?
3. Why was barrenness a burden for Hannah and how did she respond to her condition?
4. Why did Peninnah become Hannah's rival?
5. What were some of the challenges faced by women in polygamous marriages?
6. How did Hannah respond to Peninnah's harsh treatment?
7. What kind of priests were Hophni and Phinehas? How did their behavior negatively influence the worshippers?
8. What was Eli's response to his son's behavior?
9. How did the Lord vindicate Hannah?
10. How does Hannah's prayer compare to Mary's Magnificat? (Read 1 Samuel 2:1–16 and Luke 1:46–55).
11. Why was it important for Hannah to keep her vow to the Lord? (Ecclesiastes 5:5)
12. What was the significance of Elkanah's response to Hannah's vow?
13. What did Hannah do to prepare Samuel for his role in the tabernacle?
14. What lessons do Hannah teach us about motherhood?
15. What is the difference between praying and "crying out" in prayer?

## Behind Door Six
## Leah: Comforted by Her Children

> So Leah conceived and bore a son, and she called his name Reuben; for she said, "The Lord has surely looked on my affliction. Now therefore, my husband will love me."
>
> Genesis 29:32

"What are you doing?" I asked Rachael. "I came to ask you for some of your son's mandrakes. I hear that Reuben found some in the field." Replied Rachael. "Oh, really?" I said. "You have taken away my husband now you want to take my son's mandrakes too?" Rachael retorted, "*Your* husband? That is a laugh. The only reason that you were given to Jacob in the first place is because age trumps beauty." I shook my head in disgust and said, "Oh that is a low one—even for you Rachel. How dare you mock me you fruitless bride; your paps have never given suck! You stay away from my son!" Rachael was angry. She pointed her finger and said, "Fruitless bride! Fruitless bride? Jacob does not love you—he loves me! The only thing you are good for is bearing children. Besides, I have children now, from Bilhah." I sneered back, "Yes, by your maid Bilhah—but not from your womb. What have you given Jacob for a heritage? Your womb bears no fruit. You have no children. How many maids will sit on your knees to bear your children—*Rachael?*"

Then Rachel looked at me with tears in her eyes and said, "Leah, why are you striving with me? What harm have I done to you my Sister? Am I the cause of our plight? Our father brought you to Jacob by trickery on what was to be my wedding night. We have both been exploited for our father's gain!"

"You have well said my Sister; for I had no intention of going into Jacob's bedchamber before you. Is it not enough that Jacob despises me and you are loved? Is it not enough for you to have *beauty* and favor, and I am unlovely and weak in form? I have nothing to give Jacob but children—would you take that away from me too? The humiliation and hurt I feel when he goes into your bedchamber is unbearable at times. I hear your laughter; and I see the pleasure on Jacob's face when he looks at you. As for me, I have been *robbed* of my dignity. There is no room in Jacob's heart for me. I am but a means to an end—an entrapment and constant reminder of our father's deception. How dare you stand there to take away my mandrakes! Not a word Rachel—not one more word!" I am Leah, and this is my story.

## When Jacob Arrives

We lived in Paddan Aram, a place near Haran, where Abraham the patriarch lived before God sent him away from his kindred to Canaan. God promised to bless Abraham's seed, but his wife Sarah was barren. Sarah was well advanced in years when the promise was finally fulfilled. When God opened Sarah's womb, she bore a son and called him Isaac, because God made her laugh (Genesis 21:6). After Sarah's death, Abraham sent his servant to find a wife for Isaac from among his kindred—for he did not want Isaac to marry a wife from among the Canaanites. When the servant returned, he brought Rebekah, the daughter of Bethuel, son of Nahor—Abraham's brother. So Isaac married Rebekah, Laban's sister; and he was comforted after his mother's death.

Isaac was forty years old when he married Rebekah. He loved Rebekah but she was barren. So Isaac prayed to the Lord on her behalf and the Lord blessed Rebekah with twin sons, Jacob and Esau. Just as his father Abraham, Isaac did not want his sons to marry Canaanite women. So he sent Jacob to Paddan Aram, to the house of our grandfather, Bethuel, to marry a daughter of Laban (Genesis 28:1-2). Our father told us stories about Abraham, Sarah, Isaac and Rebekah. The stories were fascinating but many of the details were missing. When Jacob arrived, he filled in all of the gaps. He told us many things, including why he really left home. This is how it all began.

One morning, Rachel went to the well to water our flocks. I remained home to do the chores around the house. When Rachel returned, Jacob was with her. We were all so excited to meet him. It had been a long time since a relative, especially a near kin, had visited. Jacob was a stranger to us. We had never met him. We later learned that Jacob was fleeing from his brother Esau because he had stolen his birthright. Our father told us many stories about his sister Rebekah—how beautiful she was and how he had not seen her since she left with Abraham's servant to marry his son Isaac. Therefore, it was no small thing that Rebekah's son Jacob had arrived at our home. That day, many cherished memories of Rebekah were spoken of in our home.[1] What a welcomed joy Jacob was to our father. So Jacob remained at our house for a month.

I watched Jacob gaze at Rachel. She was so beautiful and he was undoubtedly captivated by her lovely form. Jacob loved Rachel from the moment he met her. I believe that he stayed much longer just to be near her. When Jacob came to us, he came empty. He had no money. Therefore, Jacob made an agreement to work for seven years as a dowry for Rachel to be his wife (Genesis 29:18). My father was delighted, and I . . . well . . . I watched these things unfold from a distance. For my father was not always one to be trusted.

For the next seven years, Jacob lived with us. His love for Rachel grew and she too loved him—in her own way. Our affection for Jacob grew as the days went by because he was much like Laban; shrewd, charming, and yes, the dynamics of the relationship between my father and Jacob were interesting, and at times quite provocative. Both my father and Jacob tested each other's wits, as they were both crafty men. Nevertheless, as time went on, they began to deal fraudulently with each other, which revealed a family trait that each of them had to come to terms with.

## Our Father's Deception

Seven years marched by. Season after season rolled away and Jacob had become more like a son to Laban than a man working for his bride. One day Jacob said to Laban, "Give me my wife. My time is completed, and I want to lie with her." (Genesis 29:21). I listened closely and discretely to their conversation. Would there be a wedding? Will my sister be married soon? What did this mean for me? I was torn. A part of me was happy and a part saddened. I am the eldest, not the beautiful one. Perhaps I was even a little jealous. Rachel, my beautiful sister would soon be a bride.

There was a feast that night. All the men were gathered and Laban made sure that the wine was plentiful. There was food, laughter, singing and dancing; a celebration that lasted until late in the evening. We pampered the bride while the men celebrated. Rachel was beautiful and excited. We helped her prepare for her wedding night and in spite of my inward struggle, I wanted it to be perfect for her. By the end of the night's celebration, all of the men were full of wine and some were even a little intoxicated. Then the awful happened.

I was awakened and rushed into Jacob's tent. My father instructed me to keep quiet and lay still. "No my father, this should not be." The words were in my mouth, but I could not speak! I gazed at my father in the glow of the moonlight hoping that he would read the desperation on my face, but he silenced me and told me to lie down and cover myself. I could not defy my father's wishes, so I did as I was told. Jacob lay with me that night and I became his wife.

There is some dysfunction in every family. Nevertheless, my father's actions were well below any reasonable expectation of a father. Instead of protecting us, Laban placed us in the midst of his scandalous scheme—all because he wanted to improve his financial condition. He gave no thought to the impact this deception would have on Rachel, Jacob, or me. I was placed in a difficult position. But, I had no choice but to obey my father. I could not shake the eerie feeling that somehow I willingly participated in this deception. Could I do such a thing? I still struggle with the events of that night. Some might believe that I wanted it this way. But it was never my intent to come between Rachel and Jacob. Well . . . I guess that God will judge us all.

The next morning when Jacob discovered that he had lain with me instead of his dear Rachel, he was furious! After all, Jacob was not at all a young man. He had worked seven years for his bride and looked forward to consummating their marriage. Jacob honored his agreement with my father only to be cheated out of the bride he labored seven years to wed. Of course, Laban gave him a flimsy excuse. It was *really* a lie! He told Jacob, "It is not our custom here to give the younger daughter in marriage before the older one." (Genesis 29:26).

I felt nothing but shame and guilt as I listened to our father's conversation with Jacob. That I would be a part of such a despicable plot was repulsive. How could I face my dear sister? Rachel would be devastated. It hurt to hear Jacob complain of not having the bride whom he loved. Imagine my disgrace. I lay with a man who was betrothed to my sister. "Our custom! Where is that written?" I knew of no such custom. My father secured another seven years of labor by exploiting Jacob's love for Rachel. He made light of his deception and instructed Jacob to "Finish out this daughter's bridal week; then we will give you the younger one also, in return for another seven years of work." (Genesis 29:26). The insensitivity and cruelty of my father's deception speaks to his wicked character. "This daughter's bridal week?" He refers to me as "This daughter!" Then, he refers to Rachel as "The younger one!" What had we become to our father, a bargaining chip for free labor! To make matters worse, Laban had the audacity to convince Jacob to work seven more years for Rachel. Yes, perhaps in the beginning Rachel was too young for marriage, but our father's deception was never justified. From that moment on, the relationship between Jacob and Laban was embittered. Jacob agreed to the new terms, but our house was filled with tension and my relationship with Rachel was strained—to say the least.

## Finding Comfort in My Children

In silence and darkness, I entered Jacob's bedchamber. Jacob's night of wine drinking and celebration impaired his ability to discern that I was not the bride that he worked seven years for. In the morning light, I became one of the cruelest plots of deception imaginable. As was our custom, the marriage feast lasted seven days. What should have been a time of feastings and celebrations was overshadowed by a cloud of disappointment and resentment. Jacob was confused and deeply frustrated by Laban's betrayal. What's more, I had to come to terms with my duplicity. My actions toward Rachel were hurtful; and Jacob, well . . . he showed little interest in me as his bride.

Jacob went through the motions of finishing out the bridal week. As soon as the week was completed, Jacob went in to Rachel. What was even more disgraceful is that Laban lured Jacob into the sin of polygamy.[2] Polygamy is degrading and humiliating; it creates a great deal of suffering and emotional anguish for women. I had to endure Rachel's bridal week just as she had to endure mine; and Laban went on as if nothing was wrong. Some people can be so entrenched in sin, selfishness, and immorality, that they become insensitive to the heartache their actions cause others. That was Laban. He was selfish and shameless and as long as he got what he wanted, he cared nothing about the impact his actions had on his family.

For the next several years of our lives, Rachel and I were at odds with each other. I suppose, under the circumstances, Jacob was as much of a husband to me as he could be. Still, I genuinely loved Jacob and wanted to be a good wife to him. So, I did everything I could to please him and to turn his heart toward me. But Jacob loved Rachel, and all of his affections belonged to her. Then it happened. I was with child. I was the first to bear Jacob a son—Reuben was born! I thought, surely, Jacob would love me now, only to discover that love is a matter of the heart. We can do nothing to cause someone to love us. We cannot earn it, we cannot force it, and we certainly cannot demand it. Jacob's heart was for Rachel; he only tolerated me.

I found a great deal of comfort in Reuben for several reasons. The most important reason was that God had looked upon my affliction. I knew that God was with me, especially in the moments when I felt insecure or unappreciated because I lacked beauty. Nevertheless, God balanced the scales of Rachel's beauty and my unloveliness by granting to me what every woman in my culture wanted—a son! Though I had no honor in my marriage, God bestowed upon me even greater honor through childbearing (1 Corinthians 12:23–24). For the next years, God blessed my womb with sons—Simeon, Levi and then Judah. Nevertheless, Jacob's heart never turned in my direction. Still, I praised the Lord—for in spite of my longings for Jacob's affection, God was gracious to me. I may have been blemished on the outside, but the fruit of my womb gave me legitimacy as a wife!

Although Jacob loved Rachel, she was barren. For all the time that I bore Jacob sons, God closed Rachel's womb. Jacob's love was no longer enough to console Rachel. The tension between us began to increase. Rachel was bitter and envious. She was so desperate for a child that she began to press Jacob sore. She commanded Jacob to "Give me children, or I'll die!" (Genesis 30:1). What Rachel did not understand is that only God can open and close a womb. Rachel's hope was in Jacob, so she pleaded with him to give her children. Nevertheless, my hope was in the mercy and providence of God Almighty. After Judah was born, God closed my womb and I stopped bearing children.

## The Bitter Rivalry and Competition

It has been said that true love deepens into companionship.[3] I deeply regret that Jacob never loved me enough to become my companion. Likewise, with all of the distractions of our polygamous relationship it is doubtful that Rachel and Jacob became *companions* in the truest since of love. As time went on, my relationship with Rachel deteriorated into a bitter rivalry and competition for not only Jacob's affection but also in childbearing. Rachel was desperate to have a child, so one day she came to the decision of offering her maidservant Bilhah to Jacob so that she could build a family through her. As Polygamy gained more acceptance, many barren women began having children through their maids. Jacob went in to Bilhah and Bilhah conceived a son for Rachel—he was called Dan, because Rachel said, "God has vindicated me, he has listened to my plea and given me a son." (Genesis 30:6). I was not happy that Rachel bore a son through her maid Bilhah because I had a sinking feeling that Jacob's heart would never turn toward me now. Rachel believed that she would prevail by having children through her maid. Therefore, she gave Bilhah to Jacob again and she bore him Naphtali. Well, if it worked for Rachel, perhaps it would work for me—thus, the bitter competition began. Since I had stopped bearing children, I offered my maid Zilpah to Jacob and in the course of time, Zilpah conceived, and Gad was born.

There is nothing more pathetic than two women vying for the affections of the same man. Not only did the competition between Rachel and me degrade us, it also took a toll on Jacob. We pulled Jacob deeper into the conflict between us; and now, he had other wives to consider. Our children were also negatively influenced. The values that they learned by watching us formed their character so much so, that even Reuben got involved in the childbearing competition. One day, while playing in the wheat fields, Reuben found mandrakes and brought them to me (Genesis 30:14). Mandrakes were often called aphrodisiacs because of their narcotic influence on sexual desire and powers to induce fertility. We called them "love apples" in the ancient world.[4]

What a great sin my sister and I committed out of jealously and our uncontrolled desires for Jacob's acceptance and affection. I even stooped to the level of bargaining with Rachel to "hire" my husband to lie with me in exchange for my mandrakes (Genesis 30:16). The frustrations and anguish of our polygamous marriage and depravation of affection in my relationship with Jacob caused our home life to erode into a place wrought with competition, jealously, and bitter rivalry. For the next years, Rachel and I continued to trade our husband for children. Issachar was conceived out of the wages I paid Rachel with the mandrakes. My sixth son was called Zebulun, but Jacob never loved me in return. After my daughter Dinah was born, I stopped bearing children. Throughout all of the sin and bitter rivalry between Rachel and me, God remained faithful and gracious toward us. God opened Rachel's womb and she conceived and bore a son; she named him Joseph because she said, "God has taken away my disgrace." (Genesis 30:18–24).

## Jacob Longs for Canaan

Jacob lived in Paddan Aram for twenty years, and now he longed to return to the land God had given to his ancestors. Jacob's body was in Paddan Aram, but his heart was turned toward Canaan, the land of his father Isaac. After Joseph was born, Jacob went to Laban and asked leave of him so he could take his family and return to his own place and country (Genesis 30:25–26). I knew that Laban would never allow such a thing. He enjoyed the blessings God bestowed on him through Jacob too much to give him leave. His livestock had increased, his wealth had increased, he had sons and daughters, and now he had grandchildren—his quiver was full (Psalm 127:3–5). Laban was content. He had used Jacob for all these years; surely, he would never consent without devising a scheme that would benefit him the more. Indeed, he tried, but this time Jacob outwitted Laban!

Jacob persuaded Laban to allow him to provide for his wives and children by giving him all the spotted sheep, speckled goats and all the brown lambs for his wages (Genesis 30:32). Jacob was cunning. He knew what he was planning. But Laban was so caught up in his scheme to convince Jacob not to leave; he missed what Jacob was *really* up to. God honored Jacob's labor and in the course of time, the discolored flocks grew in number while Laban's flocks became scrawny and weak. Laban never understood Jacob's knowledge of flocks and cattle, which he brought with him when he fled to Paddan Aram from Canaan. Jacob's wealth increased. His sheep and cattle were strong and robust. Jacob added even more servants and herds to his possessions—including camels and donkeys. He became exceedingly prosperous, while Laban's wealth dwindled. Laban became angry and his countenance toward Jacob became hostile! When my brothers began to complain, Jacob knew that his time in Paddan Aram must end so he called a family meeting.

Rachel and I met Jacob in the field and he told us all that was in his heart (Genesis 31:4–15). We all knew that Laban was angry because an air of resentment filled the house. Therefore, we agreed to return to Canaan with Jacob. I knew that God was with Jacob and that Jacob listened to God. I was certain that we would leave our father's house and depart in safety.

It was during sheepshearing time when Jacob rose early and packed up to leave. Laban was away shearing his sheep, so there were no good-byes or blessings for the journey. Jacob knew that Laban would never allow him to go in peace, so we gathered all of our belongings, including our livestock and all that Jacob had gained, and left for Canaan. Unbeknown to us, Rachel stole Laban's idols and hid them among her belongings. We were on the third day of our journey when Laban discovered that we had left home (Genesis 31:22). It took Laban seven days to catch up with us, and he was furious! He claimed that he pursued us because of the stolen idols, but there was much more to it than that. He even accused Jacob of taking us captive because he could not believe that Rachel and I would leave willingly. My father set a trap for Jacob that lasted over twenty years and now the seeds of deception were in full bloom, and Laban did not like his crop!

We were resting in the mountains of Gilead when Laban caught up to us. He was careful with his actions toward Jacob and held back his rage, but his words betrayed him (Genesis 31:29). I watched as my father stood there—grasping for any reason to justify his evil schemes and to deny Jacob's departure. Nevertheless, Jacob stood firm. Laban's wickedness was no match for all the good that God had done through Jacob. That day, God humbled Laban before Jacob—for Laban could not stand against what was right with any dignity. As I listened to Jacob's discourse, I felt guilt for my part in Jacob's pain (Genesis 31:36–42). In the end, Laban conceded, and the two men made a covenant before the Lord. They took stones and erected a pillar and a heap of stones. We ate there and Jacob called it "Galeed" which in the Hebrew language means, "watchtower." Laban named the place "Jegar Sahadutha," a "heap of witnesses," so that neither of them would pass beyond the heap nor the pillar for harm (Genesis 31:51–52).[5] Jacob offered sacrifices of peace offerings, and we ate and remained on the mountain that night. Laban arose early the next morning. He blessed us and kissed us goodbye. My father looked worn and sad; I welled up inside with emotion. I felt so sad as I watched him leave—I regretted all that had happened—I would miss my father. I glanced at Rachel; still, she held on to the idols.

For all the time that he dwelled in Paddan Aram, Jacob was faithful to Laban. When Jacob arrived in Paddan Aram, he had nothing. He was a deceiver, a trickster, and true to his name, he was much like his uncle Laban. Despite all of that, God changed his heart, his character, and even his name. I watched the transformation of Jacob and the honor he held before Laban. Jacob's heart had finally turned toward God.

## Our Brief Encounter with Esau

I was reminded of my position as Jacob's wife as we made our trek through the land of Seir—the country of Edom where Jacob's brother Esau dwelled (Genesis 32:3). Jacob was afraid of Esau. He had not seen him since he stole his birthright and fled to Paddan Aram. Jacob feared that Esau would fulfill his threat to kill him if he ever saw him again. So, Jacob sent messengers ahead to greet Esau. Nevertheless, when the messengers returned they told him that Esau was coming to meet him, and that he had four-hundred men with him (Genesis 32:6). I have never seen that much fear in a man's eyes. Jacob was so afraid. He prayed fervently that night. The next day, he divided us into groups so that when Esau attacked one group another group might flee to safety. Of course, I was placed in one of the groups ahead of his beloved Rachel.

Jacob sent the servants ahead with donkeys, herds of cattle, sheep, and goats—as a peace offering for Esau (Genesis 32:13–16). He instructed the servants on what to say to Esau. That night, Jacob lodged in the camp. The next morning we all crossed over the ford of Jabbok, but Jacob remained on the other side of the stream. We waited for him but he did not come until morning. When Jacob entered the camp, he had a limp, but more than that, something else had changed.

Esau finally caught up to us. He was a red man, not what I expected at all. His appearance was rugged and wild. It was evident that Esau was a man of the field; he was strong and robust, not at all like Jacob. Esau's reaction to Jacob shocked everyone. It was clear by his greeting that Esau had forgiven Jacob long ago. He lighted off his horse—hugged and kissed Jacob, and they wept. How much time had these men lost over a wrong that was never made right! How sad it is for us to quarrel with our relatives only to discover that there is nothing more precious to God than relationships. I thought of Rachel that day and longed for things to be the way they were before Jacob came.

We departed and went on to Bethel and settled there for a while. Jacob trusted God and made us rid ourselves of the foreign gods. He built an altar to the Lord, and buried the foreign gods and rings under the oak at Shechem (Genesis 35:4). Rachel conceived and bore Jacob another son, but the delivery was hard, and she died giving birth to Benjamin. We buried Rachel on the way to Ephrath. Oh how I miss my dear sister. I regret that we lost so much time competing and quarrelling over Jacob. Alas, that time is lost forever. My deepest regret is that I can never go back and recapture the loving friendship and fellowship that was lost so long ago. We finally made it to Canaan and lived out our days in the land Jacob loved. Jacob was a new man; he was now called "Israel." God's promise to Israel was secure and he delivered in an amazing way. God blessed Israel and showed that he is indeed an incredible God!

## The Lessons

There are so many lessons to be learned from the dynamics of my family. Laban and Jacob were both dishonest men. Perhaps, the only difference between them is that Jacob repented. The character flaws of my father—the culture in which we lived—and the values formed in our household caused much of the discord in our home. To be sure, every family has some dysfunction in it. It may be cultural, environmental, or caused by patterns and lifestyles of sin and disobedience. It may be a combination of all of these things. Therefore, we must be careful to turn our hearts toward God, repent of our sins, and strive to eradicate the patterns of immorality and the sins, which can influence the future generations of our children.

## Focus on your Inward Beauty

The first lesson is to focus on your inward beauty. Much of our attention is drawn toward outward appearances. Rachel possessed an allure and natural beauty that was rare among women in Ancient Israel. Nevertheless, God is not concerned about our outward appearances as much as the inward beauty of a woman with a meek and humble spirit (1 Peter 3:3–4). Our bodies are breaking down and degrading with time. Thus, we must not be preoccupied with our outward appearance. Inward beauty is precious in the sight of God, for people look at the outward appearance, but God looks at the heart (1 Samuel 16:7). One cannot impress God with one's looks. After all, he created us; and we are fearfully and wonderfully made (Psalm 139:14). God intricately designed every detail of our being. We must never compare ourselves to others or focus on what is lacking in our appearances, especially according to man's standards of beauty. Everything that God made is good. Build up within yourself qualities of wholesomeness, purity, grace, peacefulness, love, and the fear of the Lord. Remember, "Charm is deceptive, and beauty is fleeting; but a woman who fears the Lord is to be praised" (Proverbs 31:30). Seek qualities that are important to God rather than man.

## Be a Godly Mother

The second lesson is, be an example of godliness for your children. We must be careful of the examples we model before our children. Children learn more from what we do rather than what we say. Reuben was about seven-years-old when he brought the mandrakes to me. My son got involved in helping his mother to compete with his aunt in childbearing. What are our children learning from our behaviors? What quality of character are we building in our children based on what we do? It is important for us to teach them the ways of God and to model before them examples of godliness, purity, holiness, honesty, faithfulness, and righteousness. We must teach our children to fear God; to honor the Lord with their labor, and reverence his name, because the fear of God is the beginning of wisdom—and the foundation of our faith (Proverbs 1:7). As godly mothers, we must train our children in the *way* that they should go, so that when they are old, they will not turn from it (Proverbs 2:6).

## Value your Relationships

The third lesson is that we must value our relationships. Jacob and Esau were estranged for over twenty years because Jacob stole

Esau's birthright. Nevertheless, as time went on, Jacob and Esau finally resolved their differences. But so much was lost—fellowship, kinship, the joy of being around family. It was similar for Rachel and me. We fought and competed for the love and affection of one man. Certainly, the circumstances of our marriage to Jacob were beyond our control. However, we had a choice; we could love and support one another or engage in bitter battles of jealously, envy, and competition. What did we gain from all of it? When Rachel died, I realized how petty and foolish we had been. I would have given anything to have her back. All that time is lost—I can never get it back. I buried the love I had for my sister deep in the mire of striving for the affection of a man whose heart never turned toward me—no matter what I did. Love does not envy; it seeks the well-being and good fortune of others. Envy is an attitude of hostility. Rachel was more beautiful and more loved than I was. I was jealous and felt unattractive and unwanted. Nevertheless, my love for Rachel should have caused me to overcome my feelings of inadequacy. True love causes us to desire the best for others and share in their favor rather than compete with it.

Finally, relationships are important to God. Our sins separated us from God and sinful man could do nothing to make amends for himself. We were destined to die; but God demonstrated his love toward us, by sending his only begotten son, Jesus Christ, to die in our place (John 3:16). God expressed unconditional love toward us, even while we were in our lowest state of depravity. He sent Jesus to die in our place because our relationship with him was more important than the sin that separated us.

## Study Questions

1. What character flaws did Laban and Jacob have in common?
2. What impact did polygamy have on the relationship between Leah and Rachel?
3. How did Leah and Rachel cope with feelings of inadequacy, rejection, and low self-esteem? What should they have done?
4. What qualities of beauty are important to God?
5. How did God balance the scales between Leah and Rachel?
6. How did the strife between Leah and Rachel influence Reuben's behavior?
7. In terms of parenting, why are parent's behaviors more important than their words?
8. How did Jacob seek to restore his relationship with Esau?
9. What was the turning point in Jacob's life?
10. Why do you think Jacob and Esau wept when they saw each other again?
11. Why was it important for Leah and Rachel to make peace with each other?
12. Based on this study, what lessons have you learned about relationships?

## Behind Door Seven
## Esther: A Queen for Such a Time as This

"Go, gather together all the Jews who are in Susa, and fast for me. Do not eat or drink for three days, night or day. I and my maids will fast as you do. When this is done, I will go to the king, even though it is against the law. And if I perish, I perish."

Esther 4:16

"Let go of me Haman! Get your hands off me!" I shouted. "No my queen you must listen to me. Queen Esther, I beg you—if I may have but one word with you—please before the king returns. Please my queen, do not turn me away!" "I am not your queen!" I retorted. "Get away you vile dog. Let go of me. You desired to destroy my people and me, only because Mordecai would not bow down to you, as if *you* are a god. You are despicable Haman. You are a wicked man. Now let go of me. Your pride will be your undoing. Your heinous plot has now turned on you and you will die by your own hand. Let go of me right now or I will scream!" Haman pleaded, "Please . . . please my queen . . . listen to me. I beg you—please hear me out. I . . . I am desperate for your mercy my queen. Please speak to the king—for he is determined to do evil to me. Queen Esther, only you can save my life!" I glared at Haman, "How dare you plead for mercy when you showed no mercy towards me or my people; only death and utter annihilation was in your wicked heart and now you plead for mercy? There will be no mercy for you Haman—just as you showed no mercy for the Jews. Now . . . get off my couch!"

When the king returned he was furious. He shouted, "Haman! Haman! What do you think you are doing? Get away from my queen. Remove your hands now! Get your hands off her. Will you not molest my queen while she is with me in my own house?" Haman cried out in desperation, "Oh, no my lord. No . . . not I! You must listen to me my lord. I would never harm the queen. The king sneered at Haman, "Listen to you? Guards, take him! Get this vile man out of my sight—seize him now! Take Haman and hang him on the gallows that were built by his own hands." So they covered Haman's face and took him away. I am Hadassah, and this is my story.

## Queen Vashti's Audacious Defiance

There is a great evil in boasting of one's great power at the expense of exploiting others—especially the poor, the weak, and the defenseless. This was the case with the supreme rulership and authority possessed by Ahasuerus, also called Artaxerxes, the king of Persia. The Jews were exiled from our beloved Jerusalem and held captive by the Persian Empire. The vastness of the Persian Empire was almost incalculable; it stretched from India to Ethiopia and consisted of 127 provinces. There were 127 princes leading these provinces, and as massive as its wealth and supreme rulership, the sin, oppression, corruption, and moral decay of Persia was even greater! Nevertheless, Persia, in all her glory had peaked and was now slowly losing its supreme rulership and preeminent powers.

In the third year of his reign, King Ahasuerus gave a banquet to commemorate his power and rulership over the great Persian Empire. All of the nobles, princes, military leaders, officers and hundreds of dignitaries were invited, and for 180 days the king displayed before his guests all the splendor and glory of his majesty (Esther 1:2–4). Throughout the festivities, the king impressed his guests by showing his royal treasures and flaunting the magnificence and power of his kingdom. The guests drank from the golden vessels and feasted on the king's banquets and delicacies. At the end of 180 days, the king gave another banquet for the people, both small and great, in the enclosed garden of the palace in the citadel of Susa (Esther 1:5). It was a grand occasion. Many tents arrayed in fine linens were erected to accommodate the vast crowds of people. As the days of celebration progressed, the wine flowed freely, the gluttonous appetites of the guests were satisfied with food and everyone was able to drink and enjoy the feast as they wished. As was the custom, Queen Vashti held a feast in her royal house for the women, apart from the men (Esther 1:9). The name Vashti means "beautiful woman" and indeed, Queen Vashti was the most beautiful woman—in face and in form—throughout all of Persia and Media.[1] Vashti was not only physically beautiful, she also modeled before the women her stately magnetism and virtues of modesty and piety.

On the seventh day of the feast, the king was filled with wine and in his drunken state wanted to excite his guests with even more tantalizing entertainment. And so, King Ahasuerus in all his braggadocios grandeur sought to impress his guests with the beauty of his lovely Queen Vashti—as if they had not already had the privilege of seeing her at other occasions. Nevertheless, the king sent seven of his eunuchs to command Vashti to appear before his guests, "wearing her royal crown" (Esther 1:10–11). But Vashti refused. In making this outrageous demand, the king placed Vashti in a difficult position—for such a disgraceful display would be a most demeaning affront to the Queen. Besides, it was against Persian laws and customs for women to appear in public without a covering. It was also against the law for the Queen to be present at feasts where excessive wine drinking and reveling was taking place.[2] As for the king, Vashti's body was for him alone. But in his drunken condition, he jeopardized his reputation as husband and protector of his wife, by attempting to expose the Queen's body before a room filled with drunken guests and strangers.[3] Out of her own sense of modesty and in submission to Persian customs, Vashti defied the king's request. That night, King Ahasuerus made several demands for the Queen to appear. But Vashti stood her ground and refused. She risked her life and took it upon herself to protect her honor since the king was too drunk to do so himself.[4]

King Ahasuerus was incensed! Vashti's defiance made him look weak and humiliated him before his guests. Here was the great King Ahasuerus in all of his splendor—one moment he was showing the vastness of his kingdom and his rulership over the great Persian

Empire—and in the next, he made a spectacle of himself when he could not control his Queen. King Ahasuerus was so mortified that he abruptly ended the feast and rudely dismissed his guests. Out of his mind with wine and anger, the indignant king summoned all the wise men and experts in the law to determine what to do to Queen Vashti for her insubordination (Esther 1: 13–15). Memucan, one of the seven nobles of Persia, warned the king that if Vashti's disobedience was made known to all the women, this could cause the other wives to despise their husbands too, "then there would be no end to the discord!" he said. (Esther 1:16–18). Nevertheless, Memucan overlooked the fact that several women were already in the presence of the Queen when she refused to present herself to the king.

After conferring with the king, a royal decree was declared and written in the laws of Persia and Media that Queen Vashti be removed from her royal position and never enter into the King's presence again! Did the wise men really have the king's best interest at heart? Perhaps, they wanted to appease the king in his angered state or solidify the husband's authority in his household (Esther 1:21–22). Regardless, the king's rash decision to divorce Queen Vashti was an even greater loss to him (Esther 2:1). In his heart, King Ahasuerus adored Vashti as his queen and wanted to be reconciled to her. After all, Vashti was one of his treasured possessions. But it was too late. King Ahasuerus made a decision out of prideful anger and when the wine wore off and his anger subsided, he regretted his decision to divorce Queen Vashti.[5] King Ahasuerus' beautiful queen was banished from his presence. In all of his greatness, he did not possess the power to restore her because the edict was irreversible. And so, Vashti was removed from her royal position as the queen and in keeping with the advice of the wise men, "another who is better than she" was sought to replace her (Esther 1:19, NRSV). Nevertheless, in all of these things, God was at work on behalf of the peoples of Israel. Thus, a decree went forth and a fair young virgin was sought to replace Queen Vashti (Esther 2:1–4).

## My Providential Appointment

I am Hadassah the daughter of Ab'-hail. My Persian name is Esther, which means "a star."[6] After the death of my father and mother, my cousin Mordecai adopted me as his own and took me in to live in his house. We lived in Susa, the capital city near the royal palace. The kingdom of Persia was massive. But the Jews occupied only a small portion of the land—we were dispersed throughout all of the provinces of the great Persian Empire.[7] This happened after the northern kingdom of Israel was defeated by the Assyrians and Jerusalem had been destroyed by the Babylonians. Israel suffered through the Roman destruction of the second temple. After that, my people were dispersed throughout the Persian Empire. The separation caused us to have no sense of our Jewish identity or even a native land to call home. In Persia, my people suffered relentless racial prejudice, bigotry, hostility, and injustice.[8]

My uncle Mordecai was from the tribe of Benjamin. When Nebuchadnezzar, the king of Babylon, defeated Judah, Mordecai's descendants were exiled from Jerusalem and held in Babylonian captivity (Esther 2:6). In the land of Persia, Mordecai became a palace official. However, he remained steadfast in his devotion to the God of our Fathers and his beloved Israel. Mordecai was a man of wisdom; he held a strong belief that the God of Israel would one day deliver us, and restore Israel to her position as a great nation. He taught me many things about God and our nation. I learned how to present myself as a woman of virtue and piety. Although I was a woman of low estate, Mordecai taught me the graces of inner beauty; things like godliness, humility, and respect. It is one thing to possess outward beauty, Queen Vashti certainly did. But God is not impressed by our outward beauty. God is interested in our inward, unfading, beauty—a gentle and humble spirit. Perhaps, that is why I gained so much favor when I was presented before the king.

A decree went forth into all of the provinces appointing officers to bring the fairest maidens to the harem at the citadel of Susa. We were to be placed in the custody of Hegai, keeper of the women. The maiden that pleased the king the most would be chosen as Queen Vashti's replacement (Esther 2:3–4). Mordecai made sure that I was among the virgins brought into the king's house for preparation. All of the maidens brought into the king's house were prepared with oils of myrrh and sweet perfumes for purifying women—it was an experience that lasted for twelve months (Esther 2:12). Seven maidens were assigned to attend to my needs. Mordecai had forewarned me not to reveal my Jewish heritage; and I was careful to obey his instructions. Mordecai never left the court of the women's house. I knew of his presence and that gave me great comfort. Mordecai made himself my protector. He was aware of my place among the maidens and walked daily before the court of the women's house (Esther 2:10–11).

Hundreds of virgins completed the purification. I watched with nervous anticipation as each night a young virgin was escorted to the king's chamber. In the dawn of every morning, the young maiden was escorted to the second house of the women to remain with the king's chamberlain Shaashgaz, the keeper of the king's concubines. She was never to be brought before the king again unless she was called for by name (Esther 2:14). As hundreds of virgins were brought before the king and returned each day, I wondered, what is the meaning of this? Ten months passed before I too was taken into the royal house and into the king's chamber. When I stood before King Ahasuerus, he was mesmerized, but I was frightened. I trembled before his presence and stood motionless, for I could not move toward him unless he granted permission. Then, he reached for me. He was very kind.

## Foiling the Murderous Plot

Mordecai was a doorkeeper and sat among the officials at the king's gate. Mordecai remained at the king's gate watching over me from a distance, while God was watching over the Jews from his holy throne. It was at the gate that Mordecai uncovered a plot to kill the king. Two of the king's chamberlains, Bigthan and Tresh, became angry with the king and conspired together to assassinate him. When Mordecai discovered the plans of Bigthan and Tresh, he sent word to me. I warned the king but was careful to give Mordecai the credit for saving the king's life. After the matter was investigated, Bigthan and Tresh were hanged for their treason. But the king never publicly recognized Mordecai for making the matter known and saving his life. Nevertheless, all that Mordecai had done, the investigation of the conspiracy, and the hanging of Bigthan and Tresh, was recorded in the chronicles in the presence of King Ahasuerus (Esther 2:21–23). No matter the good done by Mordecai, evil was continually lurking nearby and the Jews would later face an even more dangerous enemy—Haman the Agagite!

## Haman Builds His Gallows

Haman, the son of Hammedatha the Agagite, was among King Ahasuerus' most trusted nobles. Haman was a descendant of the Amalekites, one of Israel's most vile archenemies. The Amalekites were descendants of Amalek, the son of Elipaz, who was the grandson of Esau. Israel first encountered the Amalekites when they reached the Promised Land in Canaan (Exodus 17:8). The Amalekites lived as nomads. During Israel's quest to possess the Promised Land, the Amalekites roamed about and joined forces with many nations to fight against Israel.[9] The Amalekites were a stench to God, so God cursed them and declared to Moses that any remembrance of them would be blotted out (Exodus 17:14). King Saul, the Benjamite, and Israel's beloved King David, fought wars against the Amalekites. Nevertheless, King Saul lost favor with God, because when he encountered the Amalekites he spared Agag the king. One day while King David and his men were camped at Ziklag, the Amalekites raided and burned the camp. They took all the spoils, men, women, and children; including David's two wives, Ahinoam, the Jezreelitess, and Abigail the Carmelitess, widow of Nabal. But, David and his men pursued them, and God gave King David a great victory that day. David and his men annihilated the Amalekites and recovered all; not one thing was lost (1 Samuel 30:17–18).

Now, we have the prideful Haman, the Agagite, promoted by King Ahasuerus to a seat more prominent than all the princes and nobles. Haman demanded, and at the king's command, that all the people he encountered honor him by bowing and showing reverence to him (Esther 3:1–2). However, as for my dear cousin Mordecai . . . well . . . he refused to bow down to Haman. Mordecai was a patriarch of Israel. He was solely devoted to the God of Israel; so he rejected Haman. Mordecai refused to bow to any man or object other than God—he would never bow to anything that God had cursed—and certainly not an Amalekite![10] Haman was incensed! Haman hated Mordecai and Mordecai hated Haman. The other officials at the gate were afraid for Mordecai. They tried to reason with him, especially since the king commanded that all should respect Haman. Still, Mordecai refused and this infuriated Haman—even to the point of committing genocide. The officials at the gate pressed Mordecai until he told them that he was a Jew. Then it happened. One day the royal officials told Haman that Mordecai was a Jew. When Haman discovered who Mordecai's people were, he determined in his heart to destroy all of the Jews throughout the entire kingdom of Persia (Esther 3:4–6).

God commanded the Israelites to blot out the memory of the Amalekites from the face of the earth (Deuteronomy 25:17–19). Now, Haman, true to the character of his barbaric ancestry, desired to destroy the Jews. He agonized over one man's refusal—Mordecai's refusal—to bow down in reverence to him. Therefore, Haman was filled with prideful vengeance, and sought to destroy all the Jews in the provinces of the kingdom of Persia.

Haman cunningly convinced King Ahasuerus that the Jews despised the laws of Persia and observed their own laws and customs instead. It was with this reasoning that he convinced the king to destroy all of the Jews. Haman even went so far as to offer the king ten thousand talents of silver in restitution for any loss of taxes suffered because of the destruction of the Jews. Of course, this was of no expense to Haman for he planned to take the spoils from the massacre of the Jews and keep them for himself.[11] He was indeed a depraved and malicious enemy of the Jews. King Ahasuerus, with all of his inattentiveness to important matters, did not realize the extent of the damage this outrageous slaughter and massive genocide would cost his great Persia. Thus, he agreed and gave Haman the freedom to do what he pleased to the Jews (Esther 3:11). King Ahasuerus, without question, granted Haman's request and the matter was written by the scribes, sealed with the king's signet ring, and published throughout all the provinces of the great Persian Empire. The edict was written and could not be changed.

## The Great Lamentation of the Jews

When the king's decree was circulated throughout all of the provinces, there was a great lamentation among the Jews. Mordecai tore his clothes and put on sackcloth and ashes. He was so overcome with grief that he cried out in the city with a loud voice and went before the king's gate wearing mourning clothes, which were forbidden to be worn into the king's gate (Esther 4:1–4). There was weeping and wailing amongst the Jews so great that they could not be consoled. When I was told these things by my maids and chamberlains, I sent clothes to Mordecai for I feared what would happen to him if he were seen in the gate. But Mordecai was in bitterness of soul and continued to cry out.

I sent my most trusted chamberlain, Hatach, to the street and commanded him to find Mordecai. What was the thing that troubled him so? When Hatach returned he gave me a copy of the decree that was written to destroy all the Jews. My heart sank—I grew faint as I read what was published in the writing. Then, Hatach told me all that Mordecai said, including the amount of money Haman promised to give to the king's treasuries in exchange for utter annihilation of my people (Esther 4:4–7). "What? How could he!" I exclaimed.

Then, Mordecai demanded that I go in to the king and plead for the lives of my people. I could not do that. It was unlawful for anyone to enter into the inner court to approach the king unless he or she was called for. The punishment for doing so was death—unless the king holds out the golden scepter and spares his or her life. I had not seen or been called to come into the presence of king for thirty days (Esther 4:11). I could not risk my life . . . *could I?* Nevertheless, Mordecai commanded me more sternly. "Do not think that because you are in the king's house you alone of all the Jews will escape. For if, you remain silent at this time, relief and deliverance for the Jews will arise from another place, but you and your father's family will perish. And who knows but that you have come to royal position for such a time as this?" (Esther 4:12–14).

Can relief and deliverance arise from another place? But, what place? Oh, my God, these words hit me so hard! Mordecai was right. I am in this place for a purpose. I was not condemned by Mordecai's words; I was strengthened and encouraged to do whatever it takes to save my people. Therefore, I sent this reply, "Go, gather together all the Jews who are in Susa, and fast for me. Do not eat or drink for three days, night or day. I and my maids will fast as you do. When this is done, I will go to the king, even though it is against the law. And if I perish, I perish." (Esther 4:15–16).

I called a fast because I needed all the Jews to join with me in prayer that we might receive God's mercy. We all needed to purge ourselves before the Lord; to humble ourselves and bow in prayer, and to sanctify ourselves in this fast (Isaiah 58:9). So Mordecai and the Jews throughout all the provinces of Persia fasted for three days and nights. On the third day, I felt anxious as I dressed and put on my royal robes. I walked through the palace and stood motionless in the inner court of the palace—right in front of the king's hall. The king was there, sitting on his throne (Esther 5:1).

## Queen Esther's Royal Banquet

I am not sure what I had in mind to say to the king that day as I approached his throne. I only knew that I had a duty to God and my people and there was no greater cause than to lose my life but for this purpose. When King Ahasuerus held out the gold scepter, he looked pleased with me, so I gingerly approached and bowed before him and touched the tip of the scepter. "What is it Queen Esther? What is your request? Even up to half the kingdom, it will be given you." King Ahasuerus was the great ruler of Persia, but the courage in my heart came from an even greater King, my Lord—the God of Israel. God had shown me favor throughout my ascension to the throne as Queen of Persia; surely, he would be with me at such a desperate moment for the Jews. Indeed, God in all his majesty was present in the room with me as I stood before King Ahasuerus. When I faced the king, the plan became clear—it was right before me. I smiled at the king and said, "Only this, my king . . . " and I invited him to the Queen's Banquet and requested that he bring Haman too (Esther 5:1–5).

I was repulsed by Haman's presence at my table. He made small talk and tried to impress the king with his pompous wit. While we were eating and drinking King Ahasuerus asked again, "What is your petition?" To keep him in suspense and off balance, I invited him and Haman to come again on tomorrow to another banquet; and there, I would share my petition. The king agreed and so did Haman. Haman was full of himself as usual. He went out and boasted to all that would listen, of all his wealth and the honor that the king had bestowed upon him (Esther 5:9–12). He even bragged about being the only one invited to the Queen's Banquet! Haman was a great illustration of pride. Nevertheless, "Pride goes before destruction, and a haughty spirit before a fall" (Proverbs 16:18). Haman was riding high, but he was soon on his way to a great fall.

## Mordecai is Honored

I often wonder what God is up to, especially, when he does things that are ironic and yet so profound. Haman was basking in all his glory, but there was a fly in his milk . . . Mordecai! Mighty kingdoms have fallen because of the pride of one man. Friends have separated because pride was more powerful than reconciliation. Families have been destroyed because the prideful heart of husband or wife refuses to forgive. Haman was a wicked man indeed. As King Ahasuerus' most trusted and honored officers, he had everything going for himself. Nevertheless, his pride ultimately caused his demise. Haman was fixated on Mordecai, to the degree that he would murder an entire nation of people to get back at one man. That day, Haman went home dissatisfied because he hated seeing Mordecai at the king's gate. When he told his friends and his wife,

Zeresh, about his hatred of Mordecai, they advised him to have gallows built seventy-five feet high and that he ask the king to hang Mordecai in the morning. Haman's hatred of Mordecai blinded his sense of reason. Thus, he was delighted and listened to the unwise advice of his wife and his friends. Haman decided to have Mordecai hanged on the gallows on the morning of the Queen's Banquet (Esther 5:9–14).

Nevertheless, that night King Ahasuerus was restless and could not sleep. So he called for his attendants to come and read the chronicles of his reign as King of Persia. As God would have it, the attendants read the writing of Mordecai exposing Bigthana's and Teresh's plot to assassinate the king. Then King Ahasuerus asked, "What honor and recognition was done for the man Mordecai?" The attendants replied, "Nothing." Then the vile Haman entered the outer court of the palace. When the king heard that Haman was present, he asked Haman what should be done. That conceited Haman thought that the king was referring to him! So that he could gain even more distinction and admiration for himself, he came up with the most extravagant honor. This is what Haman said:

> For the man the king delights to honor, have them bring a royal robe the king has worn and a horse the king has ridden, one with a royal crest placed on its head. Then let the robe and horse be entrusted to one of the king's most noble princes. Let them robe the man the king delights to honor, and lead him on the horse through the city streets, proclaiming before him 'This is what is done for the man the king delights to honor!' (Esther 6:7–9).

At Haman's suggestion, the king commanded Haman to go at once and do these things to Mordecai the Jew! Haman's countenance fell, and his face changed to a color no one had ever seen before. But, he was careful not to let on to the king that he was mortified. Humiliated by his own suggestion, Haman grudgingly robed Mordecai and led him on horseback throughout the city, exclaiming in his own words; "This is what is done for the man the king delights to honor!" As for my cousin Mordecai . . . well . . . he enjoyed every minute of it. At that moment I realized that Haman was powerless to do us harm. For what could he possibly do? Everyone knew that Mordecai was a Jew.

## The Queen Reveals her Secret

Now that everything was prepared, it was time for the banquet. King Ahasuerus and Haman arrived, and we sat down to eat. Haman did not look too well—I supposed it had to do with the events of the day. I knew that the king was anxious to know what was in my heart, so when he asked again, I gingerly began to share all that was in my heart. "If I have found favor with you, O king, and if it pleases your majesty, grant me my life—this is my petition. And spare my people—this is my request." (Esther 7:3). I told the king all that was being plotted against the Jews, how that we had been sold to be destroyed and slaughtered throughout all the provinces! I shared how I would not have bothered the king with such matters if we were being sold as slaves—but *genocide?* I could not hold my peace.

The king was incensed, and asked, "Who is the man that would dare to do such a thing?" I looked at Haman and pointed at him, "The adversary and enemy is this vile Haman." (Esther 7:6). In a rage, the king left the room. Haman was terrified! There we were face to face and for a moment—dead silence. Then, Haman arose and leaned toward me on my couch. Pleading with me his face so close to mine, I felt sprinkles of his spit on my face. "Get off me!" I wrestled with Haman while he pleaded with me for his life. Then the king returned from the palace garden and commanded Haman to release me. The king was furious! "Will you molest the queen while she is with me in the house?" He exclaimed! Then the guards came in and covered Haman's face.

## The Jews Deliverance

Haman's heart was bent on doing evil to the Jews all because Mordecai refused to bow down and reverence him. What gall he had to believe that he, an Agagite, deserved honor at all! Out of his prideful vengeance and twisted view of himself, Haman built gallows and sought to annihilate an entire nation of people, but the violence he sought to do against the Jews was done to him. That very night, Haman was impaled and hung on the very gallows that he had prepared for Mordecai. One must be careful not to set traps for the innocent for it is written, "If a man digs a pit, he will fall into it; if a man rolls a stone, it will roll back on him." (Proverbs 26:27).

After Haman was hung on the gallows, I told the king of my heritage and that Mordecai was my cousin. When Mordecai came into the presence of King Ahasuerus, the king removed his signet ring, the one he had retrieved from Haman's finger, and gave it to Mordecai. The king awarded me Haman's entire estate. I placed Mordecai in charge of Haman's property, his wealth, and all that he owned. What irony! Mordecai was now in control of the estate of the Jews worst enemy, Haman the Agagite! But the Jews were not out of danger; the edict written to destroy all of the Jews was a law and could not be reversed! Once again, I implored King Ahasuerus to save my people by overruling the law written to destroy the Jews. The king granted my request, and Mordecai and I wrote the edict on behalf of the Jews and sealed it with the king's signet ring. The decree was written into law by the royal secretaries.

In the days and weeks that followed, the Jews wrought a great victory over their enemies throughout all the provinces of Persia. King Ahasuerus granted the Jews the right to assemble and defend themselves against all armies or any force that would seek to do harm to us. In every province throughout all of Persia, there was joy and gladness—and the Jews rested in the presence of God.

## The Lessons

My life is a testament to the providence of God, especially in times of distress. Mordecai was a patriot and never wavered in his commitment to God. He did not allow anyone or even catastrophic circumstances to cause him to abandon his people or to compromise his allegiance to the only true God. He taught me the virtues of obedience, honor, and courage. These virtues helped me to ascend from the lowly position of an orphaned Jewish girl in captivity, to the Queen of the Persian Empire. In the end, all of these qualities positioned me to save my people from utter annihilation. These are the lessons.

## Put On the Garment of Obedience

Mordecai taught me the importance of obeying those that have authority over you. In the midst of laws and customs that were in opposition to our Jewish culture, the values I learned at home gained me favor and placed me in a position to become the Queen of the most dominant Empire in my time. Obedience made room for me to achieve a position powerful enough to save a nation from destruction. Obedience places us in a position to be used by God for his divine purposes. Disobedience does just the opposite. Obedience requires self-denial and humility, much like Our Lord demonstrated when he humbled himself and became obedient to death—even death on a cross (Philippians 2:8).

We are more like Christ when we cast away our pride, submit to those in authority, and put on the garment of obedience. As Queen of the great Persian Empire, I submitted myself to Mordecai, even as his servant, and in doing so, glorified God.

## Put on the Garment of Honor

Honor has to do with integrity, respect, uprightness, and esteem. Not only did I obey Mordecai, but also, I honored him as one should honor their mother and father or anyone in authority. When Mordecai adopted me as his own, I transferred all of my respect for my parents to him. God commands us to "Honor your father and your mother, so that you may live long in the land the Lord your God is giving you." (Exodus 20:12). No truth is greater than this, for if I had not honored Mordecai as my father, and instead, lorded over Mordecai as Queen of Persia, my people and I would have died on the very gallows built by the wicked Haman. Honor requires that you reverence your parents or anyone in authority over you—and hold them in the highest esteem. There are no conditions for honor; one must honor one's parents even when one does not agree with them. Honor is a principle that brings long life to those willing to submit to God and the people he has placed in authority over you. My cousin Mordecai was one deserving such honor, and God placed him in my life for such a time as this.

## Put on the Garment of Courage

I was so afraid when Mordecai told me about the edict Haman induced the king to sign, that condemned the Jews to death. For a moment, I thought only of the law that prevented me from entering the king's presence. Nevertheless, when Mordecai told me all that was at stake, and I had a moment to digest what was ahead, I drew on the only strength that I knew—the sovereign King that rules all. Courage requires faith and faith is strengthen through prayer. God commands us to be strong and courageous. Whenever we face a problem that seems insurmountable, we must take courage because the Lord our God is with us and he will fight for us. It is never about us!

Courage requires not only faith, but also prayer and in some instances fasting. When the dispatchers heralded the orders to destroy, kill, and annihilate all the Jews, we fasted for three days and nights. We called on heaven to come and rescue us. When Daniel learned of the plot and the decree that was published against him, he went home, turn his heart toward heaven, and prayed three times a day (Daniel 6:10). When the three Hebrew boys faced the blazing furnace, they took courage and believed that God had the power to deliver them (Daniel 3:17). Finally, when the Lord Jesus Christ was condemned to be crucified on the cross, he prayed, and submitted his will to God (Mark 14:34–36). Our hope and trust must always be in the sovereign God of our salvation. God is always present. He indeed will fight our battles!

## Study Questions

1. Why did Vashti refuse to present herself to King Ahasuerus?
2. What values did Vashti model before the women in her court by refusing the king? What would you have done if you were in her place?
3. What traits did Esther possess that set her apart from the other virgins?
4. What inward traits did Queen Esther and Queen Vashti have in common? What do these women teach us about character versus outward beauty?
5. Why did Mordecai refuse to bow down to Haman?
6. What was Haman's greatest character flaw?
7. How did Mordecai enlarge Esther's view of her role as a Jew versus her role as the Queen of Persia?
8. What lessons do Esther teach us about honoring our fathers and mothers?
9. What was the purpose of the fast called by Queen Esther?
10. Why was it necessary for all the Jews to fast and pray? What lessons does this teach us about the power of corporate fasting and prayer?
11. Since God's name is not mentioned in the Book of Esther, what evidence do we have to show that he was present?

# Behind Door Eight
## Jezebel: The Wicked Shall Cease from Troubling

> "And also concerning Jezebel the Lord says: 'Dogs will devour Jezebel by the wall of Jezreel.'"
>
> 1 Kings 21:23

I was enraged when I heard the news. I cried out, "Jehu killed Joram and they chased down Ahaziah like a dog and killed him too! That wretched murderer Jehu. This is not the last of it. This is war. I will tear him into pieces and laugh in his face while I am doing it!" Then, I ordered the eunuchs to bring my royal robes and the cosmetics too. "Here, give them to me." I painted my face—put on eye make-up and straightened my hair. Then I ordered the eunuchs to bring my jeweled crown. "There. Place it on my head. If I die today, it will be a death befitting a queen." I knew that that murderous traitor Jehu was coming for me. I could hear the roar of his chariot barreling toward the palace gate. He always drove like a maniac, but I would be ready for that heathen. I will taunt him from the window and spit in his face when he looks up.

When I heard the roaring hooves of the horses at the gate I asked, "Is Jehu at the gate?" The eunuch replied, "Yes my queen, he is coming through." I laughed as I taunted him, "Zimri, have you come in peace?" I knew that that murderous dog did not come in peace. Nevertheless, Jehu would end up defeated like Zimri (1 Kings 16:15–20). Yes, he will know this day that I am not afraid of him or death! I cried out to Jehu again, "Jehu, have you come in peace?" I could see the contempt on his face when he looked up at the window and saw me—his defiant queen in all of her beauty—too beautiful to die today. How dare he come to judge me when he is no better than I am. Then Jehu called out, "Who is on my side? Who?" Enraged I thought, "If I could reach him I would scratch his eyes out." Then the eunuchs came and stood by my side. I sneered back at Jehu, "There are still those loyal to me, Jehu." To which he yelled back, "Throw her down!" "Let go of me you spineless, idiots!" I screamed as I lost my balance and began to fall.

Suddenly, I felt the sting of rocks from the cobblestone pavement on my face. Barely conscious, I felt warm blood oozing from my face and body. The pain was excruciating. I could not move. Then the horses began to trample me . . . Oh, so much pain I could barely breathe. "Why did I not die in an instant?" I could hear barking dogs in the distance . . . getting closer . . . growling and fighting . . . attacking. With every ounce of strength I had left, I cursed! I was so cold. I could not keep my eyes open. Then, there was nothing but sheer darkness. I am Jezebel, and this is my story.

## My Journey to Israel

I was a young princess when my father, Ethbaal, king of Sidon, sent me to Samaria to marry King Ahab, son of Omri. King Omri built the city of Samaria, and now his son, Ahab, reigned as the king of Israel (I Kings 16:24–31). It was a match made in hell, by a political alliance, not a marriage of love. My father, Ethbaal, was a supreme ruler of the Sidonians and the eminent high priest of Baal. He governed from the most prominent and powerful cities of Phoenicia, Tyre, and Sidon. The country of Phoenicia rests on the coast of the Mediterranean Sea. Phoenicians, also called Sidonians, lived in Tyre, Sidon, and in other cities along the coast of the Mediterranean Sea. We are seafaring people; highly sophisticated in maritime trade, seamanship and language. Sidonians are legendary for our great ships, extraordinarily skilled seamen and the wealth gained from trading and exporting goods including, gold, copper, and purple, and of course, the finest and most exotic spices. The seacoast of Phoenicia stretches northward from Acco, near Mount Carmel, to Arvad. Phoenicians are dark-skinned people. We curved our interests toward the sea because the land inward was very shallow. Many countries sought political alliances with Phoenicia because of her wealth and position along the coast of the Mediterranean Sea.[1]

As I made my trek toward the south and inland to Samaria, I could feel the humid sea air fade from my nostrils; smothered by the dense, dry, hot desert air. It was an arduous journey so I entertained myself by counting the things I would miss about Tyre: the Mediterranean Sea and the grand sea ships that sailed in and out of port. Oh, how I would miss the smell of the salt in the air—the sound of the roaring, rushing waters, crashing against the rocks—the noise of the exotic and predatory birds dancing along the seashore —and the hustle and bustle of the merchants as the precious cargo arrived and departed the coast. There was so much to see in Tyre, so much I would miss—especially the palace and the temple worship. I am indeed destined to become a "queen of politics" in a land, by all accounts, inferior to Tyre.[2]

The people were lined along the entrance to the palace gate as I and my entourage made our way toward the palace in Samaria. I brought 450 priests for Baal and 400 priests to serve Ashtoreth—for I would insist on building a temple for Baal worship. Of course, the priests would reside in the palace with me and eat from my table. Whatever I missed about Phoenicia, I would bring with me to Samaria.[3]

As we entered the palace gate, the people pushed each other and stared—eagerly awaiting their first glimpse at the Phoenician princess who would soon become King Ahab's queen. I could see that my mysterious dark beauty captivated them. I thought of ways I could exploit their intrigue of my mystique—for I could charm the venom out of a cobra without ever being bitten! I was indeed my father's representative. I had my father's approval, King Ahab's desire to align Israel with Phoenicia, and the force of Baal with me. Perhaps this was a match made for making the gods of the Sidonians an even stronger force in Samaria!

## My Religiosity and Devotion to Baal Worship

As a child, I heard all the great stories of Israel's God, Jehovah— the one true God. Jehovah is the one that performed great miracles and mighty acts before all of Israel's enemies. He is the God that sent the man Moses, a fugitive, to deliver his people from Egyptian bondage. I heard stories of how this God sent plagues of blood, flies, locusts and lice; plagues of boils and hail and even death to Egypt until Pharaoh relented and let his people go. Every nation feared the God of the Israelites. It was not until after Pharaoh's firstborn son was killed during the final death plague, that he released the Israelites from bondage. In spite of everything, he got angry and changed his mind. Pharaoh and his army chased after the Israelites and pinned them up against the Red Sea with nowhere to run. But Jehovah, the God of the Israelites, parted the Red Sea so that the Israelites could escape. Our fathers told us that a mighty wind blew, divided the sea, and dried the land so that the Israelites could cross the Red Sea on dry ground and onward to safety. Nevertheless, when Pharaoh and his army tried to cross the Red Sea, God sent another wind and closed up the sea. Pharaoh and his army drowned in the Red Sea, while the Israelites proceeded on their journey to the Promised Land under the protective hand of this Jehovah God!

Our fathers told us that the God of the Israelites protected his chosen people with a pillar of cloud by day and lighted their way with a pillar of fire by night (Exodus 13:22). The ancient fathers also told us that Israel's God went before them and destroyed the nations of Canaan. They said, Jehovah demolished the walls of Jericho with the blasts of trumpets blown by his priests and defeated all of the enemies of the Israelites that dared to deny them entrance into the Promised Land. I call it fables and old wives' tales—I do not believe a word of it!

As time went on, the Israelites finally captured all of the Promised Land. But, they became restless and too familiar with the people around them. They began flirting with other gods. This angered Jehovah so he allowed their enemies to defeat them in battle and he caused them to become slaves all over again. Nevertheless, Israel cried out in distress—repented of the evil—and pleaded for mercy. This God, Jehovah, showed them mercy and rescued them from the hand of their enemies. What is this thing called mercy? What would cause a great and powerful God to forgive such treason and lack of devotion? Who is this God; full of compassion and grace? I know nothing about this thing called mercy because Baal would not tolerate such rebellion!

I worship the gods of the Sidonians—Baal and Ashtoreth. Baal is the god of the lands and animals. He brings us rain and enriches our lands and animals. Baal makes our waterways fruitful and productive. He gives us strong and robust cattle for food.[4] Ashtoreth is the goddess of fertility. Joined with Baal she uses her sensual and seductive powers to make our women fertile.[5] I, unlike the Israelites, am fully devoted to Baal.

It was not long after my marriage to King Ahab that he built the temple for Baal and his consort, our mother-goddess Ashtoreth (I Kings 16:32–33). The 450 priests of Baal and 400 priests of Ashtoreth served in the temple. There were many temple prostitutes to provide exotic dances and orgies before the mother-goddess Ashtoreth. King Ahab joined in the worship of Baal and Ashtoreth and many of the Israelites worshipped in the temple and burned incense to Baal. My plans to subvert the worship of Jehovah as the one true God were fully underway. Out of fear, intimidation, lust, and confusion, the Israelites began to turn their hearts toward Baal. It was an invigorating time for me as I gained even more presence and power in the kingdom—and I would kill anyone that stood in my way—especially the prophets of Jehovah.

King Ahab was intoxicated and seduced by the worship of Baal and Ashtoreth. He was also mesmerized and distracted by my dark beauty and allure. He was weak, pitiful at times, and easily manipulated. I was sickened by his weakness; I exploited it and gained even more power in the kingdom. King Ahab had fallen far from his God and his heart was entrenched in evil. Nevertheless, the apex of his wickedness and all the evil done by King Ahab was unmatched by the evil wrought by my hands. I was truly my father's daughter, and I would go to any lengths to turn the hearts of God's people toward Baal.

## The Showdown at Mount Carmel

I first heard of that troubler Elijah the Tishbite when he came before King Ahab and said, "As the Lord God of Israel lives, before whom I stand, there shall not be dew nor rain these years, except at my word." (1 Kings 17:1). "At your word!" I would have killed him on the spot—but he fled. The sight of that Tishbite sickened me. What's more, I was angry with the king because he did nothing. Baal is the god of rain. Surely, Israel's God would not prevail. Nevertheless, it did not rain! For more than three years we suffered from one of the most extreme droughts I have ever experienced. Baal worship began to lose ground. The Israelites began to question whether Baal, the god of rain and fertility, was able to bring forth rain. After all, it *was* in the name of the Lord God of Israel that that Tishbite troubler prophesized, "There would be neither rain nor dew until *he* said so!"

The seasonal rains ceased and the crops suffered. The grounds were parched and there was no grass or provender for the cattle. I was enraged by the sight of this madness and suffering! This God of the Israelites was a mystery to me. How could people worship a God that they could not see? How could they serve a God who would cause such misery? I became incensed, so I began to kill off the Lord's prophets. I hunted them and destroyed as many of them as I could find. I was relentless in my efforts because I knew that there were prophets and a remnant of God's people in hiding, who remained devoted to Jehovah. I would not rest until I killed them all. Even that troubler Elijah the Tishbite ran away. King Ahab sent people throughout all the country to search for Elijah. He threatened to do harm to any ruler who lied to protect him. Ironically, we later discovered that that Tishbite prophet had hid himself in Phoenicia, in a town called Zarephath. "Phoenicia! Really?" Was Elijah's God making mockery of the king? I was livid!

The drought caused a dreadful famine in the land. There was no food in Samaria; the people grew weary and the animals began to become sick and weak. King Ahab summoned Obadiah, the governor of the king's palace, to go out with him to all of the fountains and brooks in the land to find grass for horses and cattle. Unbeknownst to the King, Obadiah was deeply devoted to the God of Israel and had hidden one hundred prophets of the Lord in caves (1 Kings 18:3–5). Elijah met Obadiah along the way and sent word to King Ahab to meet him. When King Ahab returned to the palace, he told me that he met Elijah along the way. Elijah accused him of disobeying God's commandments and leading God's people into Baal worship. He then told the king to gather all the people of Israel and the four hundred fifty prophets of Baal and the four hundred prophets of Asherah, who eat at Jezebel's table, and meet him at Mount Carmel (1 Kings 18:18–19). Then King Ahab told me all that happened after the prophets were assembled at Mount Carmel. This is what the king said:

> Elijah went before the people and said, "How long will you waver between two opinions? If the Lord is God, follow Him; but if Baal, follow him (1 Kings 18:21). But, the people answered not a word. Then Elijah said to them, "I am the only one of the Lord's prophets left, but Baal's prophets are four hundred and fifty men. Get two bulls for us. Let them choose one for themselves, and let them cut it into pieces and put it on the wood but not set fire to it. I will prepare the other bull and put it on the wood but not set fire to it. Then you call on the name of your god and I will call on the name of the Lord. The god who answers by fire—he is God."
> Then all the people said, "What you say is good."

Elijah said to the prophets of Baal, "Choose one of the bulls and prepare it first, since there are so many of you. Call on the name of your god, but do not light the fire." So the priest took the bull given them and prepared it. They called on the name of Baal from morning until noon, but there was no response. They shouted, still no response. They even danced around the altar but there was no response. Then, Elijah told the prophets of Baal and Asherah to cry out to their gods to send fire and light the altar. The prophets cried out all day until noon. Nothing happened. They even cut themselves with swords and spears, but Baal did not respond. Then, that troubler Elijah taunted the prophets and made jokes, "Shout louder!" He said. "Maybe Baal is sleeping or on vacation!" Still nothing happened!

When the afternoon passed, Elijah summoned the people to gather around him. He took twelve stones, one for each of the tribes of Israel, and rebuilt the altar of the Lord that was broken down. Then Elijah placed his sacrifice on the altar, dug a trench around the altar, and poured water on the meat and the wood. They poured water from four jars on the altar, three times, until the water ran off the altar and filled the trench! At the time of the evening sacrifice, Elijah prayed to the God of Abraham, Isaac and of Israel; "Answer me, Lord, answer me, so these people will know that you Lord, are God, and that you are turning their hearts back again." (1Kings 18:37). Then, the fire of the Lord fell and consumed the burnt sacrifice. God consumed everything—even the water was licked up out of the trench! When the people saw this, they fell down prostrate, and worshipped Jehovah. They shouted, "The Lord—he is the God! The Lord—he is the God!" (1Kings 18:39). Then they seized the prophets of Baal—took them down to the brook Kishon—and slew them there!

I boiled on the inside as I listened to King Ahab's words. "Where is he?" I asked. Enraged I sent a messenger to find that Tishbite prophet and tell him, "May the gods deal with me, be it ever so severely, if by this time tomorrow I do not make your life like that of one of them." (1 Kings 19:2). But that coward Elijah ran and hid himself.

## The Stoning of the Innocent

King Ahab built a second palace in Jezreel—we lived there when we were not at the palace in Samaria. On this occasion, I came in to the king and found him sulking and pouting, refusing to eat. He told me that he spoke to Naboth, the Jezreelite, and said to him "Let me have your vineyard to use for a vegetable garden, since it is close to my palace. In exchange I will give you a better vineyard or, if you prefer, I will pay you whatever it is worth." (1 Kings 21:2). But Naboth refused. King Ahab was pitiful. I knew that he coveted Naboth's vineyard for some time, for he wanted to plant a vegetable garden there. Naboth refused to sell it or trade it because he wanted to preserve his inheritance for future generations. What a ridiculous custom! I despised the laws of Jehovah for they stripped the kings of their power and made them like weaklings among the people. In Phoenicia the king ruled and could have whatever he wanted. How dare this Naboth say "No" to the king. I comforted King Ahab. I said to him, "Is this how you act as king over Israel? Get up and eat! Cheer up. I'll get you the vineyard of Naboth the Jezreelite." So King Ahab arose and ate.

I had already manipulated my way into a position of power. I wrote letters in King Ahab's name, sealed them by the hand of the king, and sent letters to all of the elders and nobles in the city proclaiming a day of fasting. I made sure that Naboth was seated in a place of high honor, right between two depraved liars—handpicked by me of course. So my plan to murder Naboth went into motion. I would use these scoundrels to entrap Naboth. How dare he to refuse the king's request. Nevertheless, it would not be by my hands that

## Behind Door Eight – Jezebel: The Wicked Shall Cease from Troubling

Naboth would be slain. I would use his fellow citizens and their oppressive Mosaic laws against blasphemy to destroy Naboth.

My plan worked like a charm! The lowlifes I hired conspired together and in front of all the people, accused Naboth of blaspheming God and cursing the king. How delicious! The people were so outraged that they drove Naboth outside of the city and stoned him until he died. Naboth's sons were also slain so that there would be no heirs to his property (1 Kings 21:13). When it was reported to me that Naboth had been stoned, I was amused by how the people could so easily take the word of two well-known sons of Belial over Naboth—a humble and devoted follower of Jehovah. I felt even more powerful as I went in to King Ahab and said, "Arise, take possession of the vineyard of Naboth, the Jezreelite!" Sniveling like a child that had just gotten his way, King Ahab went down and took possession of Naboth's vineyard. Disgusted by the sight of him, I thought, "Now he can plant his little vegetable garden!" (1 Kings 21:15–16).

Shortly after King Ahab went to Naboth's vineyard to take possession of it, that troublemaker Elijah showed up and pronounced more evil against the king's house. Elijah said to King Ahab, "This is what the Lord says: Have you not murdered a man and seized his property? In the place where dogs licked up Naboth's blood, dogs will lick up your blood—yes, yours!" (1 Kings 21:19). That day, through the prophet Elijah, God pronounced utter destruction on the house of King Ahab. "I am going to bring disaster on you. I will consume your descendants and cut off from Ahab every last male in Israel—slave or free" (1 Kings 21:21). That Tishbite prophet even pronounced evil against me! He said, "And also concerning Jezebel the Lord says: 'Dogs will devour Jezebel by the wall of Jezreel.'

"Dogs will eat those belonging to Ahab who die in the city and the birds of the air will feed on those who die in the country." (1 Kings 21:23–24). "What madness. What out-and-out madness!" I thought. That coward ran from me. Why would I fear his words. But King Ahab was afraid. He tore his clothes and went into mourning. While he fasted and lay in sackcloth, I fumed! Why was he so afraid of that Tishbite prophet of Jehovah. Had I not destroyed all the prophets of the Lord? This Elijah only escaped me.

## The Death of King Ahab

We enjoyed three years of rest from the harassment of the Syrians. Israel had fought and won many wars against the Syrians and now enjoyed peace. There was no war until King Ahab decided that he wanted to regain control of Ramoth Gilead. So, he conspired with Jehoshaphat, the king of Judah, to go to Ramoth Gilead and fight with the Syrians. The battle was a war against the king of Israel—for Ben-Haddad sought to destroy King Ahab, even though King Ahab spared his life at Aphek (1 Kings 20:34). King Ahab was wounded in battle and died that evening at the hands of Ben-Haddad. Imagine such treachery!

Every man returned to his country. I watched as the king's body was returned to Samaria. What a pity, he could not rest until he made his way to Ramoth Gilead! I shook my head in disgust and walked away. King Ahab was buried in Samaria with his fathers. All of the prophesies spoken by Elijah in the name of his God Jehovah were fulfilled. Just as Elijah said, "the dogs licked up King Ahab's blood at a pool in Samaria where the prostitutes bathed" (1 Kings 22:38). Alas, it was so, according to the word of the Lord spoken by Elijah. Still these things meant nothing to me; for I refused to accept Elijah's God and continued to worship Baal.

## The Death of the Ruthless Queen Jezebel

After the death of King Ahab, my son, Ahaziah became king of Israel and ruled in Samaria. Israel remained torn between worshipping the God of Israel and Baal. Although, I had replaced the prophets of Baal that Elijah that Tishbite troubler murdered in the Brook Kishon, I still had not turned the hearts of the Israelites completely from worshipping Jehovah to serving Baal and Ashtoreth. Nevertheless, even with all of the losses I suffered, I remained a powerful force in the kingdom. My only regret was not killing that meddler Elijah. Somehow, he was crafty enough to elude me at every opportunity.

One day Ahaziah clumsily fell through the lattice of his upper room. So he sent forth messengers to inquire to Baal-Zebub, the god of Ekron, to see if he would recover from his injuries (2 Kings 1:2). Along the way, the messengers encountered that Tishbite Elijah, who remained relentless in his quest to destroy me and turn the hearts of the Israelites toward Jehovah. That troubler meddled again and told the messengers to return and say to the king, "Is there no God in Israel that you are going to consult Baal-Zebub, the god of Ekron? This is what the Lord says: 'You will not leave the bed you are lying on. You will certainly die!'" (2 Kings 1:3–4). I was incensed when I heard of this! Meanwhile, Ahaziah sent captains and companies of fifty men to bring that Tishbite prophet back to the palace, but the Lord God of Israel sent fire from heaven and consumed them. Surely, the people will turn to God if they heard of this—especially if the prophesy of Ahaziah's death comes true. Finally, one captain convinced Elijah to present himself before Ahaziah, and he did. That Tishbite told my son to his face that "Because he sent messengers to inquire of Baal-Zebub, the god of Ekron, he would never leave his bed and would surely die from his injuries." Ahaziah died! Since he had no son, my son Joram reigned in his stead. As for Elijah, I never heard from that Tishbite prophet again. It was as if he vanished from the earth.

With all the political power that I had as queen mother, it was lonely in Samaria. I yearned for my home in Phoenicia. Ahab was gone—Ahaziah was gone—and Joram, well . . . he was losing his mind! Joram removed the sacred stone of Baal, erected by his father, and consulted only the prophets of Jehovah. It seemed that he was working with Elijah to tear down everything that I had built. Nevertheless, Joram did not force the people to turn their hearts fully back to Jehovah. Instead, he allowed them to worship as they pleased. As for me, I worshiped Baal in the privacy of my chambers. I watched all that I had worked so hard for begin to crumble before my eyes.[6] Joram reigned in Israel for twelve years. He fought wars; defeated the Moabites, and we even survived the famine brought on by the Syrian besiege of Samaria. Still, there was no comfort for me. By now, a new prophet, called Elisha, had taken the place of Elijah the Tishbite. He became my adversary and an even greater thorn in my side.

It was a strange day for me. I felt uneasy—I had a feeling that something horrible was about to happen. Joram was recovering from the wounds inflicted by the Syrians during the last conflict, and Ahaziah, the king of Judah, had come to Jezreel to visit him. I did not know what the kings were discussing because I was never present when the kings conferred with each other. Suddenly, there was a cry from the lookout tower that Jehu, son of Nimshi, and his troops were approaching the palace gate. I thought, surely, there would be no rebellion, for Jehu was a faithful soldier in Ahab's army. As was his way, Jehu drove ferociously toward the gate. "Is there news" I thought, as I peered at him from my window. The king sent horsemen to meet Jehu to inquire if he came in peace. But, all the horsemen sent by the king joined Jehu's army. Jehu continued to approach the palace aggressively. Then Joram and Ahaziah rode out to meet Jehu (2 Kings 9:17–23). I could see them talking to each other on the plot of ground that king Ahab stole from Naboth, the Jezreelite. Then, Joram fled! "Treason!" I cried, but it was too late. Jehu drew his bow. He pierced Joram between the shoulders—and they took him from his chariot and threw him like a wounded dog onto Naboth's field. I was furious. But what could I do? Surely, that traitor Jehu would come for me.

After some time had passed, I was warned that Jehu was returning to Jezreel. "Will he torture me too? Well, I will be waiting—I will die like a queen!" I sneered at the eunuchs. I dressed in my finest robes and painted my face. As I approached the window, I thought of myself as the dark princess of Phoenicia. Perhaps I could seduce him with my dark beauty. Then I looked down at Jehu's ugly face. He looked up at my window and cried out, "Who is on my side? Who?" My eunuchs stood next to me. Jehu yelled, "Throw her down!" The eunuchs grabbed me. I resisted but they overpowered me—and they threw me down! (2 Kings 9:32–33).

## The Lessons

I learned everything about worship, life, and living from my father Ethbaal, King of the Sidonians. I remained zealous in my worship of Baal and in my loyalty to my country until my death. It is an abominable thing to profess an allegiance to a god—as in the case of the Israelites, and not remain steadfastly devoted to that God. When I arrived in Samaria, Israel was already entrenched in idolatry. In the words of the prophet Elijah, they were "Halting between two opinions." They wavered in their faith in Jehovah, worshipped the golden calves set up in Bethel and Dan, and set up shrines to detestable idols in the high places—all of which gave place to Baal worship. I exploited their weaknesses. Nevertheless, Jehovah was faithful, even to an idolatrous people. I would have succeeded in turning an entire nation's heart to Baal worship had it not been for a remnant of God's prophets—the ones whose knees never bowed down to Baal and whose mouths never kissed him. (1 Kings 19:18).

The God of the Israelites proved repeatedly that he was the one true God, but I never accepted it. I was so entrenched in evil, witchcraft, and idolatry that my heart was hardened to the truth that Jehovah is God. I was wicked to the core. I was never converted. Alas, I died without knowing Israel's God and King—the Sovereign Lord and Creator of the universe. What a tragedy. I have a place in history—but not among the pure in heart. My legacy will always be evil. These are the lessons.

## Choose Whom You Will Serve

The first lesson that I learned, although too late, is that Jehovah reigns! When the Israelites conquered the Promised Land, Joshua reminded the tribes of Israel, at Shechem, of all that the God of Israel had done for them. Then he challenged them to "Fear the Lord and serve him with all faithfulness." (Joshua 24:14). Joshua commanded the Israelites to destroy all the gods worshipped in Egypt by their ancestors and serve the Lord. The Israelites agreed to throw away all the idols and declared that they would serve the Lord (Joshua 24:16–18). But, as time went on, they slipped into idolatry and the message of Moses, Joshua, and all the prophets of God began to fade. As a result, the people of God became enmeshed in a world of religious confusion and idolatry.

Conversion takes place in the heart. Elijah fought against the evil of idolatry in his day, just as pastors and ministers today are pleading with God's people to turn away from sin and turn back to the Lord God Almighty. Each of us must take an introspective look into our hearts and judge the reality of our relationship with God. Are we serving the Lord God Jehovah or are we worshipping the gods of this world? What will be your legacy? Will it be one of evil or will you be numbered among the pure in heart. You must choose this day who you will serve.

## Wisely Choose Your Battles

The second lesson is that you must wisely choose your battles. I fought against the Lord's Prophet Elijah because I abhorred the message the God of the Israelites sent through him. I wanted to overthrow the religion of the Israelites and impose Baal worship on God's people. From birth, I was indoctrinated into Baal worship, and I remained zealous in my convictions. Thus, I never conceded to what was happening around me. I ignored the miracles, the truth Jehovah sent through his prophets, and even the signs and wonders. Perhaps if I had submitted to the truth, I would have had a better end. Instead, I ignored all the signs because I wanted to have my way.

Selfishness is a dangerous attribute. My heart was so hardened by my need for political and religious power, that I rejected the power of Jehovah. I was blinded by my corrupt and depraved mind. At every turn, I fought against Elijah—not realizing that I really was fighting the Holy God of Israel, who has all power! When we war against the Lord's prophets, we are in essence waging war against God. I declared war against Jehovah when I destroyed all of his prophets and sought to force Baal worship on the Israelites. The lesson is that we are no match for Jehovah. Ask yourself, "Am I rebelling against God?" Are you rejecting God's Word because you do not like the message? Disobedience is evil. "Rebellion is like the sin of divination, and arrogance like the evil of idolatry." (1 Samuel 15:23). I was entrenched in both rebellion and idolatry. A war against God is a battle you cannot win. Thus, you must wisely choose your battles. I fought against the only true and living God—the Lord Almighty—and I lost.

## Choose to Live by God's Word

The final lesson is that you must live by the power of the Word of God and not by your own power. I used my powers of seduction and my political acumen to gain control in the kingdom, which should never have been mine. It was my duty, as the queen of the royal court, to submit to the Word of the Lord sent through the prophets and respect the headship of King Ahab, regardless of his ineptness, for by doing so I would have submitted myself to Jehovah. Instead, I took license to serve my own wicked ambitions and it cost me my life. There were many opportunities for repentance, but I ignored them all. God sent his words of warning through his prophets. My depraved mind and murderous acts led to a terrible end for me. I was never able to overcome my insatiable desire for power or my need to control King Ahab. I discovered too late that the Lord God Jehovah rules from the heavenly places—and no one is able to stand against him. Alas, with all the power I possessed, I eventually collapsed under God's judgement. My hardened heart led to my ultimate demise. I never repented of the murderous and evil sins I committed against God and his people. God's mercy was right at my grasp, but I refused to accept it. I struggled to gain my own power through idolatry, intimidation, witchcraft, prostitution, and even murder. All I needed was the power of the Word of the Lord. I discovered too late that the Word of God sustains us and give us life. My end must never be your end. There is no God in heaven but Jehovah!

## Study Questions

1. In what ways do parents influence the religious practices of their children?
2. What role did politics play in Jezebel's marriage to King Ahab?
3. What impact did Ahab's marriage to Jezebel have on the Israelites?
4. How did Jezebel's acts of rebellion influence King Ahab and her children?
5. Why was Jezebel so relentless in her pursuit to destroy God's prophets?
6. What did the stoning of Nabal reveal about the condition of God's people Israel?
7. Why did God destroy King Ahab's entire family?
8. What motivated Jezebel to destroy the Lord's prophets and to seek to kill Elijah?
9. Why was it so difficult for Jezebel to believe the Word of the Lord? (Read John 6:35–36).
10. Why do you think the Lord allowed Jezebel to do so much damage before he judged her?

# Behind Door Nine
## Naomi: Surviving the Storms of Widowhood

> But she said unto them, "Do not call me Naomi; call me Mara for the Almighty has dealt very bitterly with me. I went out full, and the Lord has brought me home again empty."
>
> Ruth 1:20–21 NKJV

My mind was flooded with racing thoughts as we made our trek toward Bethlehem in Judah. I was restless most of the night and all morning. I felt uneasy, doubtful, unfocused, and weak. I thought, "Is this the right thing for these women? How can I take them with me? They are foreigners—Moabite women. What will happen to them? I have nothing to offer them—not one thing left!" Ruth and Orpah were walking a few paces ahead of me, holding hands, and talking. I called out to them, "Ruth, Orpah! Come—sit. Let us rest for a while. The journey is long, and we must preserve our energy." My eyes welled up in tears as Ruth and Orpah sat and looked inquisitively into my face. They looked so young and innocent. "What is wrong, mother?" said Ruth. They always listened; well, most of the time. They are my daughters-in-law and I have come to love them dearly. But, this must be done. I stared at them and said, "You have been good to my sons and good to me; you are my daughters and I love both of you, but now we must part ways. This journey is not for you. I am an old woman now. I have nothing left to offer you. My life is bitter. I must go back to my home in Bethlehem and die in peace among my people. Look, you have your youth, your families, and your gods. You are young, beautiful women and you have so much more to give. You must return to your people. I realize now that I cannot take you to Bethlehem with me—there is too much uncertainty. My daughters, you must return to your people. Go home. Return to Moab. I will be just fine; I can make it alone on this journey. My God will take care of me!"

 Oh, how we wept at that moment. I cannot say for how long. We just held on to each other and wept bitterly. Then Ruth cried out, "No mother! Please, let me come with you. I cannot bear to part with you." "No, my daughter you must go." I replied. But, Ruth held on so tightly I could barely catch my breath. "Orpah, take Ruth—Ruth please let go—Orpah, help me with Ruth. Please, listen to me my daughters." I pleaded. But Ruth refused and cried out again, "Mother, I beg you, please let me go with you!" I looked at Orpah—she seemed so confused. I pleaded with her again, "Orpah, help me." Then, Orpah tried to pull Ruth away but she held on so tightly that Orpah lost her balance and fell backwards. Exhausted from crying and pleading, I conceded. I looked at Orpah and said,

"Orpah—go on my dear." Then Orpah stood slowly, gathered her things, and kissed my face. I smiled weakly, nodded, and gave her my silent blessing. As Orpah began to walk back toward Moab, I said to Ruth, "Ruth, see how Orpah is gone back to her people and to her gods. You must let go and return with Orpah; catch up with her my dear." Still, Ruth held on to me the more and cried, "Mother, do not force me to leave you—I will go with you and live with you and your God will be my God. Let nothing but death separate you and me."

As we sat on the ground, I held on to my dear Ruth and rocked her until her sobs turned into a soft whimper. Through my tear-filled eyes, I watched Orpah as she slipped away into the distance like a mirage. Over the hill she went—then I saw her no more. That made me so sad. I whispered under my breath, "Good-bye my dear Orpah. May the gods of your fathers be as kind to you as you have been to this old woman." Then, wearied from crying, we picked ourselves up and gathered our things. Ruth and I held on to each other as we headed toward Bethlehem in Judah. I am Naomi, and this is my story!

## My Arrival in Bethlehem

It was a thirty-mile journey from Moab to Bethlehem in Judah, so I had plenty of time to think.[1] I reflected on my life with Elimelech and all the reasons he gave me for leaving Bethlehem. There was a severe famine in the land. Although we had faced many droughts and famines in the past, somehow, for Elimelech, this one was different. Elimelech decided that we would have a better chance of survival if we made the journey to Moab where there was food.

That was so many years ago—and for me—much of the time spent in Moab was lonely and bitter, at best.

Elimelech was from the Tribe of Ephraim. He was a good man. His name means, "God is King." It was a difficult decision, but Elimelech wanted to protect his family from starvation.[2] I trusted Elimelech and believed that he knew what was best for our family. Still, since his death, I have questioned whether leaving our home in Bethlehem for Moab was the right decision; for in the days of old, Jehovah's anger burned against my people because they intermarried with the Moabites and worshiped Baal of Peor (Numbers 25:2–3). Besides, Moab has always had an adversarial relationship with Israel (Judges 11:18). Perhaps, if we had trusted God and stayed in Bethlehem, things would have been different.

After Elimelech died, it was difficult for me to live in Moab alone. Yes, I had my sons, but they could never fill the void left by my husband. I missed Elimelech. For me, widowhood was miserable and lonely. I missed the joy of Elimelech's companionship, his priestly wisdom, and the comfort he gave in times of uncertainty. Most of all, I missed the security a husband brings to one's life, especially at my age and in my culture. But Mahlon and Chilion were with me and God forbid, they both married Moabite women. What could I do? We were in a foreign land, and Mahlon and Chilion were of age. I did not have the strength to engage in that battle. Not many years later, Mahlon and Chilion died also. In my grief, I wondered if God was angry with me. My family was gone and there was nothing left for me in Moab. I had Ruth and Orpah, but they were my daughters-in-law and I could not remain in Moab. How could I die in a pagan land away from my home and my God? I worried about what would become of Ruth and Orpah—how could I leave them in Moab.

When I heard that there was food in Bethlehem, I decided to return to my home. Bethlehem seemed so distant—almost like a foreign land. I felt detached from my God and my people. When I left Bethlehem, I was full. I had a husband and two sons. Now, when I return home, I will return empty. I have no husband, no children, and no land. I was afraid. Every tie to Moab was gone; Elimelech, my sons, Mahlon and Chilion—there was nothing here for me now. My last days would be bitter because even the hand of the Almighty was against me. My mind was flooded with so many memories and questions about my future. I wondered, "Did God shorten my sons' lives because they married Moabite women? Where would we go? How can we survive? What would become of Ruth? Would they reject her too?"

When we entered the gates in Bethlehem, everything looked worn and tattered from the hardships, but recognizable just the same. As I looked at the people, I could see many familiar faces. Yes, they were older, but I recognized them. My heart was moved as I began to remember my life in Bethlehem, and I began to cry. I was overcome by my emotions. Just then, people began to recognize me—they rushed over toward us. I held on to Ruth, but it was difficult during the press as one woman after another hugged me and cried out my name, "Naomi!" Somehow, Ruth let go. I could barely see her through my tears as she was swallowed inside the crowd. She desperately reached for me, but the crowd separated us.

The women cried out my name, "Naomi, Naomi! Is this Naomi?" (Ruth 1:19). In a moment of distress, I cried out, "Do not call me Naomi; call me Mara for the Almighty has made my life very bitter. I went away full, but the Lord has brought me back empty. Why call me Naomi? The Lord has afflicted me; the Almighty has brought misfortune upon me" (Ruth 1:20–21). The crowd was silenced by my outburst. Then, Ruth was there. My dear Ruth, she was always there to comfort me. She grabbed my hands, pulled me in to herself and held on, comforting me as we walked through the crowd.

## The Provision of Almighty God

It was the beginning of the barley harvest when we arrived in Bethlehem. All the men worked in the fields to harvest the grain. As the stalks of grain were gathered, the poor were allowed to enter the fields and glean the stalks of grain that were left behind—for God commanded that the corners of the fields and some of the gleanings be left for the poor and the strangers (Leviticus 23:22). Early the next morning, I explained the gleaning laws to Ruth. Ruth volunteered to go into the fields to glean for food. I was worried that she would be greeted with hostility. Nevertheless, I agreed because we needed food and there were no other alternatives. I cautioned her to glean only on the edges of the field and prayed for her before she headed out toward the fields.

When Ruth returned later that evening, she was excited! She told me how she had gleaned in the field of a man of great wealth and how he instructed her to remain in his field, close to the young women (Ruth 2:8–9). "What did you do, my dear?" I gingerly asked. "I fell on my face and bowed to the ground and said, 'Why have I found such favor in your eyes that you notice me—a foreigner?'" Replied Ruth. Then, Ruth told me all that happened to her that day; how the man had shown her great kindness and told her what was spoken to him about her treatment of me. She told me how the man blessed her with these words, "May the Lord repay you for what you have done. May you be richly rewarded by the Lord, the God of Israel, under whose wings you have come to take refuge." (Ruth 2: 12).

Hope is a glorious thing! Hope and thankfulness is what I felt as Ruth told me all that happened to her that day. While Ruth talked, my soul began to awaken after being dead for so many years. My sadness and grief was replaced with joy—for I was refreshed by the words of hope spoken by Ruth. It had been so long since I felt the presence of the Almighty—and now I sensed that his face was turned toward me once again! My dear Ruth brought home nearly an ephah of barley. That evening we ate the food given to her by this kind man. After we had eaten, I had to ask, "Where did you glean today?" I was curious about such kindness. (Ruth 2:19).

Ruth replied, "The name of the man I worked for today is Boaz." When I heard these words, I thanked God for the favor he granted to Ruth and blessed Boaz for his kindness. I knew this was the hand of God at work in our lives. Such things do not happen by chance. Only by divine providence did Ruth glean in the field of Boaz—a near relative. God's hand was upon us. He showed his great mercy toward Ruth, the Moabite foreigner. As for me, my burden was lifted, my empty cup was at last being filled again, and the distance between my God and me was now resolved. In that place and at that moment I felt accepted by God—comforted by him—forgiven by him—and most all, truly loved again. Oh, what blessings restoration brings! I rejoiced and delighted in the Almighty for his everlasting goodness and mercy. There is nothing more to be desired than to be loved by God and in a right relationship with him. As for Ruth, perhaps the God of Israel would truly be her God, and my people would become her people. My worries about Ruth began to fade. Nevertheless, I knew that I must instruct Ruth in the ways of conducting herself before my people; for this thing was very delicate.

## My Instructions to Ruth

Ruth gleaned in Boaz's field until the end of the barley and wheat harvest. Her modesty and industry was noted by all the Israelites—especially Boaz. Most of all, God's favor was upon her; for she had done a good thing in coming to Bethlehem and caring for an old woman like me. God delights in those who show respect for the elderly (Leviticus 19:32). Now, it was time for me to do my part.

In ancient Israel, the aged women are honored and admired because they possess knowledge and wisdom far more superior than young women do. When the time came, the aged women would gather the young women and teach them how to conduct themselves as wives and mothers. These times of instruction cultivated nurturing relationships between the old and young, bridged the gap between generations, and demanded godly accountability—which enabled the young women to carry on the spirit of the same teachings to their children and the many generations to come. This is how we preserved our history, culture, traditions, and our family heritage; but most of all, this is our way of maintaining our faith and devotion to Jehovah. Now it was time that I did this with Ruth, for she came from a pagan culture, and pagan women were vulnerable to abuse and easily tempted to commit unsavory acts for survival.[3]

My husband Elimelech was a kinsman of Boaz. In our culture, there was an obligation to extend help to every relative in need. Thus, Boaz and our other kinsmen owed a duty to my husband to preserve his heritage and posterity. Since Ruth was widowed and childless, our next of kin—or the relative next in line—was obligated to buy my property, marry the widow of Elimelech's seed, and give children. All of this was designed to preserve our inheritance and in keeping with Jewish law.[4]

Ruth and Boaz's attraction to each other had more to do with mutual respect and admiration for the noble character that they possessed, rather than the flesh (Ruth 2:8–13). From the day that he noticed her gleaning in his field up until now, Boaz had shown Ruth much kindness. He took notice of the relationship that we shared. He admired her virtue, modesty, the kindness in her heart, and he was impressed by the sacrifice Ruth made by leaving her homeland in Moab to take care of me. Boaz was not just a wealthy man, he was a *go'el*, that is to say, a close relative with the power to redeem my land and even marry Ruth (Deuteronomy 25:5–10).[5] I knew in my heart that not all of these things happened by chance. The providence of God was at work and now the time was right to teach Ruth how to propose marriage to Boaz.

At the end of the harvest season, the men would go to the threshing floor to winnow the grain. The men had much to celebrate for the harvest was great. They worked late into the evening winnowing barley on the threshing floor (Ruth 3:2). After eating and drinking, they would retire for the night and sleep near the wheat. I was careful to share these things with Ruth. I said,

"Wash and perfume yourself, and put on your best clothes. Then go down to the threshing floor, but do not let him know you are there until he has finished eating and drinking. When he lies down, note the place where he is lying. Then go and uncover his feet and lie down. He will tell you what to do." "I will do whatever you say." Ruth answered. I felt anxious as I watched my dear Ruth make her way to the threshing floor. She was so vulnerable—so innocent—and so brave. She believed in what I said and I wanted no harm to come to her. "Oh, my God, please be with her." I prayed. I did not rest well that night. I worried about Ruth's safety and questioned if I had done the right thing for her.

Early the next morning Ruth came home and told me all that happened. She told how she quietly uncovered Boaz's feet and lay on the threshing floor, just as I had instructed her. She excitedly told me how Boaz was startled and asked, "Who are you?" I hung on every word. "I am your servant Ruth. Spread the corner of your garment over me, since you are a kinsman-redeemer." She said. "Oh, you did so well my child!" I exclaimed. Then Ruth explained that there was another kinsman-redeemer nearer than Boaz and how Boaz said he would take care of the matter. Boaz was very kind to Ruth. He protected her virtue by making sure no one saw her on the threshing floor. Early that morning Boaz made sure that Ruth did not return empty. He poured six measures of barley into her shawl and sent her on her way. (Ruth 3:10–15). As for me, the Lord poured an abundance of optimism in my heart that morning. I was reassured that I had done the right thing for Ruth and it was well with my soul. I knew that Boaz would not rest until the matter was settled.

## The Kinsman-Redeemer

Boaz went to the town gate and waited for the kinsman-redeemer who was next in line to buy my property. As was our custom, he took with him ten elders of the town, and the men gathered at the gate to discuss the matter. Only the kinsman-redeemer who was next in line had the right to buy my property—he also had an obligation to marry Ruth. Since Ruth had no children, the Jewish law required the kinsman-redeemer to preserve the inheritance of Elimelech's seed, namely Mahlon, my eldest son (Deuteronomy 25:5–6). I was concerned that the kinsman-redeemer, who was next in line, might not be as kind to Ruth as Boaz was. Nevertheless, it was in God's hands now, so Ruth and I waited to see how the matter would be resolved.

Ruth learned many lessons that day. She learned how the Jewish laws and customs governed our lives and protected the poor and destitute from losing their inheritance. She saw how the men made legal and binding decisions at the gate and learned the significance of leadership in our culture. Most of all, Ruth learned how to trust in the unseen God in whom she declared to make her God. As for me, as these events unfolded, I whispered this prayer, "Lord God Almighty, let these things be according to your will." There was no doubt that God had sustained us throughout our journey to Bethlehem and I trusted that he would be with us until the end of days.

When Boaz emerged from the gate, he held the sandal, which was a symbol of the transfer of Elimelech's property to himself. It was now legal! In earlier times, transfer of property takes place when one person took off his sandal and gave it to the other (Ruth

4:7). I supposed that the kinsman-redeemer next in line had too much to lose—for if Ruth conceived and had a child, Ruth's child would inherit all of the property of Elimelech and Mahlon. When Boaz announced to the elders and the people that he had bought the property of Naomi and Ruth, the Moabite widow of Mahlon, I could hardly contain myself. "It is finished!" I shouted. Everyone rejoiced. Then the elders and all the people at the gate blessed Ruth and Boaz (Ruth 4:11–12). It was too wonderful for me. I was ecstatic as I witnessed the providence of the Almighty at work in my life. That day my soul was revived. I said, "Do not call me Mara, I am Naomi, for I have found joy and my strength is renewed in the Lord. The pleasantness of Jehovah is my song, for I am redeemed!"

Boaz and Ruth were married and Ruth conceived and bore a son and called his name Obed, which means "A servant who worships."[6] The whole town rejoiced and prayed for the house of Boaz and Ruth (Ruth 4:14). Jehovah is an awesome God! I left Moab empty, now I am full again. All the women blessed God for the kinsman-redeemer, for my grandson Obed, and for Ruth. She *was* better to me than seven sons! (Ruth 4:15). The Lord did not allow this old woman to become destitute. What God did for me, he does for all of the widows who put their trust in him. God cares for the downcast. He is concerned about the widows and the orphans. I lost my two sons to an early death, but now I had a grandson. God gave me another chance to nurture and teach my grandson the things of the Lord God Almighty (Proverbs 22:6).

Boaz performed the role of kinsman-redeemer to secure the property of Elimelech. Nevertheless, there is a Redeemer mightier than he is. Boaz and Ruth gave birth to my grandson Obed and through Obed's seed came Jessie, the father of King David.

Forty-two generations later out of Obed's seed, came forth the King of kings to redeem the world from sin. His love, mercy and sacrifice led him all the way to Calvary where he took the sins of the world upon himself and redeemed us from destruction and death. He is the God of our salvation. He is the Son of God and his shed blood is the new covenant. No longer is the sandal the legal document of redemption, the Cross of Calvary is. The Kinsman-Redeemer of the New Testament is our Savior; he is the Lord Jesus Christ!

## The Lessons

There are some things that happen in our lives for which we have no control. I lost everything in Moab. Nevertheless, regardless of what I lost, as I look back to that time, I am sure that leaving Bethlehem was God's divine plan for our lives. Ruth forsook all to follow a God that she knew nothing about. She left her home, kindred, and her gods to care for an old woman and to live among people with a history of hostility toward the Moabites. Nevertheless, Jehovah rewarded her for her faith. Whatever you are holding on to, release it and place your burdens into the hands of the living God. Along this journey, what matters the most are our relationships with God and each other. We cannot make it alone. We need each other. We need prayer and support when we go through our struggles. In the midst of every trial, we must remind each other to trust in the Lord. Our hope must be built on the power, presence, sovereignty, and faithfulness of Almighty God. Encourage one another with these lessons.

## Believe in the Providence of God

When you are confused about the heartache that you are experiencing, know that God is present in every circumstance of life (Psalm 139:1–18). God is concerned about every detail of our lives. His divine presence is always with us. When you are hurting, lonely, or experiencing unbearable loss, just believe in the providence of God. There are times in our lives when the circumstances surrounding our decisions are leading us directly to the place where God wants us to be. The first lesson that I learned from all that I had lost is to trust and believe in the providence of God. Suffering is a part of life. Sometimes we must lose everything that is important to us in order to see how truly amazing God really is. My view of God's presence and power over the circumstances of my life was very limited. I depended on Elimelech, my two sons, Mahlon and Chilion, and the life we built in Moab. When they all died and everything I loved was gone, I saw myself as an old woman with nothing left to offer or even to live for. I felt that my life had ended, and it was time to go home to Bethlehem and die among my people. But, the Almighty had a greater plan for my suffering. Never forget that in our darkest moments, God is always present and he is working out his plans for our good. He is aware of everything that happens to us and sometimes, God orchestrates the circumstances of our lives to bring forth his divine plan. God is sovereign—everything in his creation is subject to him. He does whatever he pleases, and no man can stay his hand (Job 23:13).

God made provisions for Ruth and me long before we entered the gates in Bethlehem. His divine favor was upon Ruth and he made sure that we were never without shelter or food. The providence of

God led Ruth to work in Boaz's field. God touched the heart of Boaz and turned his eyes toward Ruth. God's providential will directed the dialog between Boaz and the other kinsman-redeemer and led them to his predetermined end. The Providence of God is at work in all of our lives—not fate or chance. Even when we err, God is able to use our mistakes to accomplish his divine purpose. God is in control and in all things God works for the good of those who love him, who have been called according to his purpose (Romans 8:28). If Elimelech had not taken us to Moab to escape the famine, my two sons would not have married Moabite women; and Ruth would never have been a part of my life, nor would she have blessed me with my grandson, Obed. Though I lost my husband and my two sons, I gained so much more. My faith was strengthened. My dependence on God was greater than before, and this old woman was enlivened and given purpose again!

## Believe in Your Usefulness to God

The second lesson that I learned is that as long as we have breath and health, we are useful to God. When I left Moab, I thought that my life was over. I was an old widowed woman—I was impoverished—and I was worn out. I had lost everything. My husband and my two sons were dead. I felt that I was being punished for my disobedience, and my God's face was turned against me. I only had Ruth, and she was a foreigner. I felt useless, hopeless, and I was miserable. Like many of the elderly, I felt I had nothing to offer and should sit in a corner, out of the way, and wait for death. Then something happened. Ruth clung to me. When we arrived in Bethlehem, Ruth volunteered to glean in the fields behind the harvesters (Ruth 2:3). What could I do? Then it dawned on me, I could teach her. Sometimes we are so distracted by our problems that we forget what God has called us to do. God has given the older women the assignment to teach the younger women what is good (Titus 2:3). Ruth was vulnerable. I had the wisdom to instruct her in the ways of my God and my people. So I taught Ruth how to conduct herself in the fields and even how to propose marriage to Boaz. As the years went on, I taught Ruth our customs and laws. I instructed her on how to love her husband and children. I taught her how to submit to Boaz and take care of her home. In the same manner as I was taught, I taught Ruth to be busy and self-controlled. Through all of my struggles, my greatest joy and privilege was the influence I had on my grandson Obed—even in my old age. No matter how old you are, God can use you. He has instructed us to train our children and to use the wisdom and knowledge we have gained in our winter years, to nurture and encourage the younger women. As long as we have breath and strength in our bodies, God has work for us to do.

## Believe in the Power of Friendship

The final lesson that I learned is to believe in the power of friendship. There will come a time when true friendships will be difficult to find. The world will pressure us to embrace values like "self-sufficiency" and "independence" and lead us to believe that depending on others is a sign of weakness. Nothing could be more untrue. We need each other. When we release our pride and allow ourselves to be vulnerable, we show character traits like humility, honesty, and genuineness. I was uncertain about my future in Bethlehem. I was afraid, frail, and heartbroken. The only thing I was sure of is that I did not want to die in Moab. I knew that the journey back to my homeland would be difficult, especially for an old woman like me. Nevertheless, I was determined to go home and die among my people. My pride almost cost me the most precious friendship two women could ever possess. But that day on the road back to Bethlehem-Judah, Ruth taught me a valuable lesson about friendship.

I needed Ruth and Ruth needed me. Our strengths and weaknesses combined helped us to survive the arduous journey to Bethlehem and enabled us to persevere—with minimal resources, and an uncertain future. Ruth clung to our relationship and was willing to leave her home and all that was familiar to her for the unknown. She demonstrated the most admirable qualities one could ask for in a relationship—devotion, loyalty, and love. Ruth was a beautiful young woman and still marriageable. Yet, she willingly sacrificed her personal comfort and an almost sure future in Moab to care for an old woman like me. That is the power of friendship! I realize now that Ruth was not only my daughter-in-law; she was my loyal friend.

Friendship is the ability to "companion the soul of another" and to be "readily available" to help the person you call your friend.[7] For me, friendship meant that I had to become fully transparent about my weaknesses and vulnerabilities. I had to let go of my pride, humble myself before God, and accept the help that Ruth offered. True friends stand by each other—no matter what. They help each other get through life's most difficult circumstances. Ruth and I did that for each other. Ruth used her youthful strength to glean in the fields so that we might have sustenance for our daily needs. I used my wisdom and life experiences to help Ruth gain acceptance among my people, learn about our laws and customs, and I taught her how to secure a husband. Most of all, I introduced Ruth to my God. I taught her about his faithfulness and unfailing love toward his chosen people.

Through all the hardships, I discovered there was a purpose for my suffering. God had a plan for the redemption of humanity. Boaz, the kinsman-redeemer, and Ruth gave birth to my grandson, Obed. After Obed came the greatest Kinsman-Redeemer of all. He is the Messiah—the Son of the Most High God. It all began with Ruth's love and devotion to me as her mother-in-law and friend. Now, all that was lost is restored. All of my tears are dried and my sorrow has turned to joy. I found purpose and meaning in my old age, for which, I am truly grateful!

## Study Questions

1. When Naomi returned home to Bethlehem, why did she want to be called "Mara" instead of Naomi?
2. Why did Naomi change her mind about allowing Ruth and Orpah to accompany her to Bethlehem?
3. For what reason(s) did God forbid the Israelites to intermarry with the Moabites?
4. In what ways do we see the providence of God at work in Naomi and Ruth's life? (Read Ruth 1–2).
5. Have you ever felt distant from God? What do you think it takes to have that distance resolved?
6. Why was Boaz attracted to Ruth?
7. What lessons about friendship and devotion do Naomi and Ruth teach us?
8. How did Naomi help Ruth adapt to living in Bethlehem? In what ways did Naomi demonstrate qualities of the Titus Two Woman? (Read Titus 2:3–4)
9. What provisions did God make for widows and the poor?
10. Why is it important for us to provide for the needs of the widows and orphans?
11. What was the purpose of the kinsman-redeemer in ancient Israel?
12. How does the kinsmen-redeemer in ancient Israel resemble the Lord Jesus Christ?

# 10

# Behind Door Ten
## Mary: The Sorrowful Mother at the Cross

"When Jesus therefore saw his mother, and the disciple whom he loved standing by, he said to his mother, 'Woman, behold your son!'"

John 19:26 (NKJV)

"Mother, come quickly!" said John as he burst through the door. "What is wrong with you, John? You are scaring me." I worriedly replied. "They have taken the Lord! We were praying in Gethsemane when Judas came with a detachment of soldiers. There was a mob of the chief priests, elders, and officers of the temple guards with him. They had lanterns, torches, and weapons. Judas betrayed us, Mother. Can you believe it? Peter . . . well . . . I do not know where Peter is. He cut off one of the soldier's ears, but Jesus healed him—right on the spot. Peter ran away. We all ran in different directions; we were so frightened. Oh

### Behind Door Ten – Mary: The Sorrowful Mother at the Cross

Mother, we must hurry. No one is left. We must find Jesus. We *must* help him! They arrested him—bound him—and took him away."

I stared expressionlessly at John. "It has begun." I said. My heart started pounding—I had a hard time catching my breath. Sweat began to roll down my forehead. Then, I felt this overwhelming fear for my son. This was the beginning of the fulfillment of the words spoken by Simeon in the temple: "For my eyes have seen your salvation, which you have prepared in the sight of all people, a light for revelation to the Gentiles and for glory to your people Israel." (Luke 2:30–32). "This cannot be real . . . this just cannot be real!" I said repeatedly. But, it was as real as I was human and Jesus was deity. I knew what was to come. "But not like this dear Lord—oh, my God—not like this." I prayed. Then I took John by the hand and said, "You must be brave my son. Come; let us find the place where they have taken Jesus." I am Mary, the mother of Jesus, and this is my story.

## The Mystery of His Conception is Revealed

I cannot tell my story apart from his story—for the fabric of my life is interwoven with his life. As Jesus' mother, I have experienced the joys and victories of his miracles, and the sufferings he endured while he lived among us. Jesus was no ordinary child. The life he lived on earth was never of this world. I do not know why God found favor in me, above all women, to be the mother of our Lord; that remains a mystery. Although I am called, "Blessed and highly favored among women," I endured many burdens and sorrows as Jesus revealed himself to the world. I am honored that God chose me to give birth to our Savior, but I hurriedly admit that I am not a divine being. Although I have tried to live a virtuous life, I have a sin nature like every fallen man or woman; for it is written, "In my flesh dwells no good thing." (Romans 7:18). I am saved from eternal damnation only by the grace of God through the Lord's atoning death on the cross. I do not have the power to answer prayer, nor do I have the power to save a lost soul from his or her sins. I am a poor, humble, servant of the Most High God, chosen for God's purpose, and I have the privilege of being a part of his plan for redemption.

I was born in Nazareth, a small city in Galilee. My ancestors are from the tribe of Judah; we are in the lineage of David, one of the great kings of Israel. Nazareth was so insignificant that it was believed, by some, that nothing good could come out of it (John 1:46). People often have low opinions and low expectations of small towns and the people that grow up in them. That is why my story is so remarkable. The entire landscape of Nazareth is about sixty acres and the population only around five hundred.[1] Consequently, people did not think very much of Nazareth or the people that lived there. We were poor farmers. We lived a very simple and conventional lifestyle. Yet, nothing is insignificant or common about what happened to me or what Jesus did during the time that he walked the sands of the earth.

It happened on an ordinary day and certainly unexpectedly. An angel appeared to me with a salutation I never heard before. He said, "Greetings, you who are highly favored! The Lord is with you." (Luke 1:28). "What?" I said. I stood frozen—gripped by fear. Then, the angel told me, "Do not be afraid, Mary, you have found favor with God." "Do not be afraid, Mary—*really?*" How did he know my name? But I was so afraid my teeth were chattering. Even if I wanted to run, I could not move. Then the angel told me that I had been chosen by God to give birth to his son and I was to call him Jesus, which means, Yahweh is salvation.[2] The angel told me that Jesus would be great and he would be called the Son of the Most High. "This must be a mistake because I have never known a man." I protested. The angel explained that the Holy Spirit would come upon me and that I would be overshadowed by the power of the Most High God. The child would be called the Son of God. I paused for a moment and said to the angel, "I am the Lord's servant, may your word to me be fulfilled." Then, as suddenly as he appeared, the angel left.

After this, I hurriedly made my way to the hill country of Judah to visit my cousin Elizabeth. When Elizabeth heard my greeting, she confirmed all that the angel had said. An outpouring of praise flowed from my heart as I rejoiced over the coming of the promised Deliverer. I was amazed by this pronouncement. "Could this be real?" Yet, deep within, there was also a feeling of disquiet, as I pondered what all these things meant.

In the weeks that followed, I struggled with the circumstances of my child's conception. I feared the stigma, ostracism, and ridicule of becoming a young, unwed mother. What sane person would believe my claim of being a virgin with a child conceived by the Holy Spirit? The people will think that I am insane if I tell them that the child in my womb is Israel's long-awaited king sent by God to save his people. How would Joseph react? He could divorce me in disgrace. I could be taken to the elders and stoned to death for being with a man while still in my father's house. It was our custom—it was the law!

I agonized over telling Joseph, and when I finally did, Joseph grieved over what he perceived as my betrayal. At first, Joseph did not speak one word. I knew he was planning to divorce me, so I said nothing. I prayed for him and gave him the time he needed to decide what he would do. I wondered what would become of Joseph and me. Still, if these things were from God, surely he would make it right. Joseph was a righteous man. I suffered with him while he struggled with his decision to divorce me. Then one night, the Lord visited Joseph in a dream and confirmed the truth about the supernatural conception of Jesus. From that moment on, Joseph took me into his house as his wife, but we had no union until after Jesus was born (Matthew 1:25). Joseph and I were now on this journey together, and the mystery of Jesus' conception and all the promises and prophesies of his birth brought us closer as husband and wife. As for me, I kept all of these things hidden in my heart for they were too wonderful for any expression. Through it all, God gave me an abundance of peace; and there were so many moments as Jesus grew inside my womb that I anticipated the overwhelming joy of his coming!

## My Reflections On His Birth

Jesus was born in Bethlehem-Judea. I remember when Joseph and I made the journey to Bethlehem to register for the census. It was near the time of my delivery. The city was crowded and among the hustle and bustle of finding a place to lodge, no one gave notice to a poor couple seeking a place to meet the needs of a pregnant woman. Joseph went from lodge to lodge to find a place for us, but there was no room. The only place available was a stable. The caretaker of the inn was kind enough to allow us to lodge there, and it was there that I gave birth to my firstborn son. So much went on inside of my head that day. "Am I to give birth in a stable among animals, without the help of a midwife?" I had no experience in this; and as a young mother, I was afraid. I was uncomfortable and deeply troubled by these events. Why would God allow my child to be born like this? Joseph comforted me—he never left my side. He used his carpentry skills to line a manger with straw and turn it into a crib. When the baby was born, we wrapped him in cloths, and we laid him in the manger. Joseph was so gentle with Jesus. He always knew what to do. I closed my eyes and rested.

I was startled when the stable doors opened and shepherds appeared! They spoke not a word—they just stood there—amazed by the baby lying in the manger. Then, they bowed the knee and worshiped him. Not one word was spoken. I felt a stillness and peaceful presence in that place beyond anything that I have ever known. It was a sacred moment—a silent reverence. I remember how the shepherd's faces were smudged with dirt and sunburned from being so long in the fields. Then a radiant light shined from the manger and lightened their faces! I could see the humility, hope, and amazement on their faces as they gazed upon the baby. I felt Joseph's grip tighten as he wrapped his arms around my shoulders to reassure me that everything was all right. Then, as mysteriously as they appeared, they arose and walked slowly away, glorifying God for what they had seen. How is it that God has made these things known unto shepherds? I kept these things hidden in my heart and drifted off to sleep again.

After my purification was complete, we went to the temple to present Jesus before the Lord and offer sacrifices. An old man approached us by the name of Simeon. Simeon was a just and devout man. He was waiting for God to bring help to Israel. When he saw Jesus, he took Jesus into his arms and blessed him before God. He said these words: "Sovereign Lord, as you have promised, you now dismiss your servant in peace. For my eyes have seen your salvation, which you have prepared in the sight of all people, a light for revelation to the Gentiles and for glory to your people Israel." (Luke 2:29–32).

Then, Simeon looked at Joseph and me and told us all the reasons to rejoice at Jesus' birth, but he warned us too! He said, "This Child is destined to cause the falling and rising of many in Israel, and to be a sign that will be spoken against, so that the thoughts of many hearts will be revealed." (Luke 2:34–35). Then he turned to me and with the most ominous look in his eyes, he said, "A sword will pierce your own soul too." At that moment, I knew that there would be sorrow at some point, but nothing prepared me for the cross. An old woman was there too. Her name was Anna. She was a prophetess. She spoke about the birth of Jesus to all the people who waited for the redemption of Jerusalem. After all these things were accomplished, we departed and returned to Galilee and to our home in Nazareth.

## My Reflections on the Peoples' Unbelief

In the years that followed, Jesus grew and came into his own. In spite of all that I knew about Jesus' birth—the prophesies concerning his life—the shepherds at the stable—the visit from the Magi when we fled to Egypt, and all the miracles, signs, and wonders along the way, I was afraid for Jesus because of the people's unbelief. The citizens in Nazareth were the first to reject him. I remember when Jesus stood up in the temple and read from the scroll of the prophet Isaiah, they all marveled at first. But when Jesus said, "Today this scripture is fulfilled in your hearing," they became furious, and drove him out of town. They even tried to throw him down a cliff, but he escaped unharmed. Sadly, because of the people's hostility and unbelief, Jesus did not do many works in Nazareth. (Mark 6:1–6).

Jesus continued to teach in the synagogues, cities, and throughout the provinces and lands. He chose twelve men to follow him. They became his disciples and his companions. They were a motley crew of devoted men who left all to follow him. Throngs of people began to follow Jesus when they heard his words. His words revived the hearts of all of us who had the privilege of hearing him speak! Nevertheless, the chief priests, scribes, and the elders began to fear him. They were the worst. When the news about Jesus' mighty works began to spread abroad, the people began to have hope. Some believed that Jesus was the Messiah, the Holy One of God. But, the religious leaders were troubled as his popularity among the people began to grow. They had been in charge for so long, they feared that if they did not do something to silence Jesus, they would lose their positions and power over the people. So they began to speak out against Jesus in anger—especially after the day Jesus whipped them and drove them out of the temple.

The chief priests, scribes, and religious leaders joined forces and begin to challenge Jesus' authority. They thought of him as an unlearned, self-appointed rabbi, who dared to perform these works! Some of the Pharisees and chief priests called Jesus, Satan and Beelzebub. They tried to trick him and set him up with riddles and foolish questions, but found themselves fighting against the wind. No one could match his wisdom for he was not of this world.

They all looked like fools and hypocrites because his knowledge was too great for them. This angered them the more. Jesus proved his deity repeatedly. Unfortunately, for them, they never believed. When Jesus exposed their hypocrisy, they began to lose favor with the people; so they joined forces and began to plot to kill him. They were angry because they could not silence Jesus!

Jesus was determined to fulfill his mission. His ministry demands became so great that he seldom found time to rest or eat. He moved from township to township performing many miracles, healing the sick, feeding multitudes of the poor, and casting out demons. His voice was strong and commanding; and he spoke with authority. He even had the power to raise the dead. Jesus overruled death with his spoken word. Still, the religious leaders and many of the Jews rejected him. They labeled him as a blasphemer and tried to stone him (John 10:33). Amidst all of these things, I worried because it was becoming more dangerous for Jesus. Throngs of people were following him and many believed that he was the promised Messiah. Even so, many still doubted; especially the chief priests, scribes, and the religious leaders.

In the years that followed, Jesus' popularity grew even more. The news of his works and teachings drew crowds of people and many became his followers. The crowds became unmanageable—it seemed things were out of control. Quarrels and debates began to break out as people in the crowds began to question who Jesus was. Some believed that He was the Messiah, some were confused, and some even thought he was demon possessed or raving mad. The opposition against him from the chief priests, scribes, and the elders intensified as Jesus challenged them with even more severe rebukes. It became too much for me to bear, so I accompanied my sons and went to a house where Jesus was to plead with him to come home. I had a hard time convincing his brothers that Jesus was the Son of God. They also believed he was out of his mind.

We stood outside because there were so many people at that house we could not get close to him. When the news that we were outside finally reached Jesus, he asked, "Who are my mother and my brothers?" Then he said, "Here are my mother and my brothers. For whoever does the will of my Father in heaven is my brother and sister and mother." (Matthew 12:49–50). I was stunned by his response. Hurt even. For I realized at that moment, Jesus embraced those who would prefer him above their families; the man or woman who would leave all, wear his name and follow him, and seek to do the will of his Father. From that day forward, I never sought to interfere with Jesus' ministry again.

## My Piercing at the Cross

It was the time of the Passover. I was in Jerusalem when I heard John frantically knocking at the door. He was distraught. John rushed into the house like a man running for his life! Then he told me what happened in the Garden of Gethsemane. Nothing could have prepared me for the news John shared with me that day. John said, "Mother, they have arrested Jesus." What mother can bear to hear that her child has been arrested? I was desperate to find Jesus. "Oh my God. . . . Why? . . . What has he done?" I asked. We stood motionless—in shock at first. Then I told John to be brave, and we ran as fast as we could to find Jesus. My eyes flooded with tears. I had no idea where we were going—I just followed John.

All the things that I saw and felt over the next several hours revealed the brutality, cruelty, and evilness of unregenerate men. I vaguely remember what happened during the course of the night and in the hours that followed. There were trials during the night—hidden away from the people in the secrecy of the dark halls. Most of it is all a blur now. Nevertheless, the trials were over, and now we stood at the cross watching Jesus suffer. Jesus was celebrated on Sunday with branches of palm trees and the people rejoiced "Hosanna! Blessed is he who comes in the name of the Lord! Blessed is the King of Israel!" (John 12:13). But, in the few days that followed, Jesus was tried, beaten, and nailed to a cross—and a mob cried even louder, "Crucify Him! Crucify Him!"

Jesus was in excruciating pain, he was fighting to breathe. I looked around and saw faces in the crowd; faces of the very ones whom he healed, the people that he fed, and the ones he delivered from demons. I saw the faces of the people who witnessed his miracles. In the crowd were the ones whom he loved, the ones he defended, and the ones—who hated him, mocked him, spat on him, and sentenced him to death! All the people who Jesus was dying for, stood in the crowd; and some cried out, "Crucify him!"

I did not have the strength to look at Jesus' face again. It was too painful to watch my gentle and loving son suffer. I stood helpless while he struggled to breathe. He had lost so much blood. His face was bruised, swollen, and so bloody I could barely recognize him. Now he is alone, deserted by his disciples. "Where are they? Somebody, do something!" I cried as I held on to John and the other women. But, the voices in the crowd overshadowed my lone cries for mercy. Then, I felt compelled to reach out to Jesus so he would know that he was not alone. I looked up and cried, "I am here Jesus. I am here!" The words were drowned out by the cries of the crowds. I walked in closer and reached for him, but one of the soldiers pushed me back, and I fell to the ground. Sobbing, I noticed that my hair and clothes were covered with blood, tears, and spittle. For a moment, I was confused; how did this . . . what happened? Then I remembered that I held on to Jesus when he fell along the road. His back was bleeding profusely from all the stripes he endured. Jesus was so weak from all the beatings—he struggled to carry the cross. Then, Jesus looked down at me for a brief moment. Somehow, I knew that Jesus was no longer seeing me as his earthly mother—I was a sinner—and he was the Son of God dying for the sins of the world.

I felt faint so I reached for John. "John?" I mumbled softly. "Yes mother." He reached down and lifted me from the ground. We just stood there—helpless—watching—and waiting. Mary Magdalene and Salome stood with us, and there were other women there too. Then Jesus cried out, "Eloi, Eloi, lama sabachthani!" I tore my clothes and cried out in bitterness, "Why have You forsaken Him? Why? Where are You?" Then Jesus said, "Dear woman, here is your son" and to John he said, "Here is your mother. It is finished." He breathed his last breath and then he died. I stood at that cross, hopeless—agonizing over such a profound and senseless murder. I wailed in a voice so loud and filled with grief that I did not recognize it as my own. It was as if a spear had been thrust through my heart! Then I remembered what Simeon said to me in the temple, "And a sword will pierce your own soul too." Indeed, my soul was pierced, just as Simeon had prophesized. Then the darkness came—a fierce wind began to blow—and the earth began to shake violently. Everyone ran away, screaming, and panicking! Still, we stood and watched from afar off. I wept inconsolably.

## My Hope is Restored

I am not sure how I got there, but when I opened my eyes, I was at John's house. "Rest mother," John said as he tried to comfort me. Oh, but the poor man was so drained, disillusioned, and grief-stricken himself. I tried to close my eyes again, but my mind would not shut down. I kept seeing images of Jesus—from infancy to childhood, and at different points throughout his life as a man. Everything just ran together in my head. My mind kept racing from one thought to another. I was so exhausted, but I could not sleep. I whispered—*Jesus went about doing good, not evil.* I drifted off for a moment. Then, I was awakened by an image of Jesus' face, bloody and unrecognizable. I screamed "Jesus!" John came rushing in, "Mother!" John cried as he cradled me in his arms. He was doing all he could to comfort me, but I was so overwhelmed with sorrow, I could not be comforted. We held on to each other and wept bitterly.

In the days that followed, I sat quietly and pondered all the things that led up to Jesus' death. In fact, it seemed everyone was quiet. There was an eerie stillness in the air. I guess we all were grieving in our own ways. Although I knew that Jesus would die one day, I was never prepared for the horrific circumstances of his death—not on a cross! I felt so empty—so hopeless. As I looked through the window in the place that John made for me at his house, the lump in my throat was so big I could barely swallow. I thought, "Mary, no need to doubt now. It is finished." Then, I thought of his disciples. They are all gone now. Only John is left. All the sheep have scattered. They all must be devastated!

It was after the Sabbath and Jesus had been dead for three days. I was alone, still restless and exhausted from crying so much. What am I to do with all that has happened? What now, my Lord? What now? I thought. I knew that I needed to prepare Jesus' body for burial. I struggled with the thought of seeing him as he was in his last moments on the cross. I did not know how I could manage to get through it.

Now, it was very early on Sunday morning. Perhaps, John was still asleep. It seemed no one was stirring but me. Then, I heard a knock at the door and when I opened it, there stood Mary Magdalene with the most astonishing look on her face. I looked at Mary Magdalene as she stood at the door and then I looked beyond her and into the sky. My heart was filled with emotions so intense I could barely breathe. The *Son* was now shining and it was a glorious day! I grabbed Mary Magdalene's hand and we walked outside. Not a word was spoken between us, but deep down inside my soul I knew. He is risen! Just as he promised. Jesus Christ is risen! I cannot tell you of the overwhelming relief and joy that flooded my soul. It is well! No more death. No more crying. No more sorrow. Jesus said, "Behold, I make all things new." (Revelation 21:4–5). Everything *is* new—just as Jesus promised!

## The Lessons

From the moment the angel foretold of Jesus' birth, my life changed forever. I have experienced joys and sorrows along my journey, but through it all God has been faithful. You too may have also experienced a life-changing, earth-shattering moment; perhaps, it may be something wonderfully spectacular or even dreadful! Nevertheless, every stripe he took was for your healing. He endured every insult hurled at him to cover your shame! Jesus loves you so much that he died for you. Every nail, every taunt, and even the piercing of his side were endured so that you might be delivered from sin and have eternal life. Jesus has the power to heal every hurt and bring hope and forgiveness to even the most degrading and painful circumstances. Do not despair because Jesus is not dead. He is alive—and he is always near.

You are not alone as you navigate your way through this arduous journey and seek to make sense of your sufferings. There is a struggle behind every door. Nevertheless, Jesus can heal every hurt. Do not be afraid. Do not get weary in your struggles. Let Jesus have your burdens—he truly cares for you (I Peter 5:7). Life is wearisome for all. We all have a story to tell, and there is nothing new under the sun, for What has been will be again; someone else will experience the same or a similar challenge in his or her life. (Ecclesiastes 1:9). Someone needs to know that he or she is not alone in his or her suffering! That is why you must tell your story. You must tell others about the grace of God. You must tell another weary soldier that there is forgiveness, and there is healing through Jesus Christ the Lord.

Yes, there is a place of rest for you; the Lord *is* your Shepherd (Psalm 23). He is the great Physician—He is a Wonderful Counselor, Mighty God, Everlasting Father, and the Prince of Peace. (Isaiah 9:6b). He is the Christ, the Son of the Most High God! He bore the cross so that you might live and be at peace with God our Father in Heaven. Jesus laid his life down for you. Now you must learn to live victoriously. You must walk in the newness of life and here is how you do it.

## Follow His Example of Love

The first thing you must do is follow his example of love. Jesus said, "Greater love has no one than this, that one lay down his life for his friends." (John 15:13). Are you one of his friends? You are if you do what he has commanded (John 15:14). The love Jesus demonstrated is a sacrificial love. It is a love that seeks the good of a person, even when there is nothing received in return, and even when one does not "deserve" it. Remember, Jesus loves us, including the ones who crucified him. His love for us constrained him to pay the price that redeemed us and saved us from our sins.

God is love. Out of his divine love, he created man to have fellowship with him. But, when man fell into sin, we fell out of fellowship with God. So God sent his Son to restore the relationship between himself and fallen man. Jesus moved outside of himself and sacrificed his life to pay the price to redeem humanity. Jesus' eyes were on others and so must our eyes be on others. We all hunger after love! We need it to survive. Why not give back to others what we crave the most—love.[3] Does that mean that God wants us to sacrifice our lives to demonstrate our love for others? No, it is not in that sense. What it means is that we must love others out of a sincere devotion to God. Jesus loves us in the same manner as the Father loves him (John 15:9). As such, he commanded us to "Love each other as I have loved you." (John 15:12).

Jesus' worth is far greater than our worth. Nevertheless, he extended his love toward us—even though we are unworthy. God sent Jesus to show us an example of love that is greater than death. In light of this, we must show our love for Jesus by loving one another in the same way—unconditionally! That means, our love for others must move beyond our personal interests, pride, past hurts, and presumptions. That is the sacrificial love God expects us to demonstrate toward others.

Lastly, the fruit of our love must show up in acts of kindness, patience, long-suffering, and gentleness. Love should never be envious, boastful, proud, or rude. Love must never rejoice in evil or lies. Beyond everything that happens, good or evil, love must always persevere (1 Corinthians 13:4–7). Love is the greatest gift that God has given to humankind. Everything begins with, and builds on love. Every act of faith and kindness, every expression of joy and sorrow, every friendship and every hope, must have love at the root of it.

## Follow His Example of Obedience

Second, we must follow his example of obedience. Jesus is God. He emptied himself, took on the very nature of a servant, humbled himself, and became obedient to death—even death on a cross! (Philippians 2:6–8). There is no greater example of obedience than this. No death is more degrading, ignominious, or inhumane, than the death on a cross. Nevertheless, Jesus was willing to obey our Father and sacrifice his life for sinful humankind. We were foul, useless, abominable, and wicked creatures; in spite of that, Jesus left his heavenly kingdom and came down in obedience to his Father to rescue us from our sins. The Lord made us righteous through his atoning death on the cross (Romans 5:19).

He was a Prince but he did not enter the world with any pomp and circumstance. He was born in a lowly manger. He was a servant of the very ones that should have served him. Although, his wealth and worth was beyond all the riches of all the kingdoms of this world, he lived in poverty. In obedience to the Father, Jesus became accursed, humbled himself, and died on a cross.[4]

Now, we must respond in obedience to him. How do we obey God? We obey him with all of our heart and with all of our soul (Deuteronomy 32:46). We show our love for God when we obey his commandments (John 14:23). God makes our lives prosperous and successful when we submit ourselves to him and obey his Word (Joshua 1:8). Obedience provides us with the assurance that we will enter the kingdom of heaven (Matthew 7:21). There is an abundance of safety for those who choose to obey the will of God. Jesus said, "Therefore, everyone who hears these words of mine and puts them into practice is like a wise man who built his house on the rock." (Matthew 7:24). When we walk in obedience, our lives are secure. No matter what trials or storms we face, we have the assurance that, although we may fall, we will not be destroyed! Thus, we must honor our Lord by obeying God's commandments, even in times of distress and sufferings.

## Follow His Example of Forgiveness

The third lesson is that, we must follow his example of forgiveness. You may have been victimized by the cruelty of people or circumstances beyond your control. Nevertheless, Jesus taught us to forgive even the most heinous acts committed against us. We live in a fallen world and we are fallen people, "For all have sinned and fall short of the glory of God." (Romans 3:23). That means that we all need forgiveness. It is written, "There is no one righteous, not even one." (Romans 3:10).

If you no longer want to be bound by your past, learn how to forgive. In order to forgive we must possess the right heart. Our old, unregenerate heart must be transformed into a new heart. No one can change our hearts but God. Nevertheless, we must first turn our hearts to God. Forgiveness is more for us than it is for the one that has hurt us. We are never more like Jesus than when we reach down within our souls and say, "I forgive you." How can we receive God's forgiveness if we are unwilling to forgive someone else? Unforgiveness hardens our hearts and builds walls of bitterness. Walls of unforgiveness are fortified with attitudes of resentment, hatred, anger, and evil thoughts. Many of the physical, emotional, and mental illnesses that people experience are birthed out of a spirit of unforgiveness.

When a person refuses to forgive, it not only destroys the person who refuses to forgive, but also everyone else around him or her. In teaching his disciples to pray, Jesus said, "For if you forgive men when they sin against you, your heavenly Father will also forgive you." (Matthew 6:14). The next time that you ask the Father to forgive you, why not think about all of the people that you have yet to forgive. The question we all must ask ourselves is—Who needs forgiveness the most?

Finally, at the foot of the cross, I heard Jesus say, "Father forgive them, for they do not know what they are doing." (Luke 23:34). Even in his dying moments, the Lord's profound compassion and divine grace was at work toward his tormentors. Jesus suffered for us; he died for you and me. That is why, through all of the pain and heartache we experience, we must imitate his forgiveness.

## Study Questions

1. What kind of character did Mary possess that caused her to be chosen by God to be the mother of Jesus?
2. What worries did Mary have about the circumstances surrounding Jesus' conception and birth? How are Mary's concerns relevant for women today?
3. Why was it difficult for Mary to balance her role as Jesus' earthly mother and Jesus as her Savior and Lord?
4. Why were the religious leaders so determined to kill Jesus?
5. Traits like hypocrisy, jealousy, and envy influenced the religious leaders to plot to kill Jesus. How do these character flaws destroy relationships among Christians today?
6. The women in Mary's life were supportive of each other in times of struggles. What lessons about friendships and relationships do these women teach us?
7. What lessons have you learned because of your study of Mary the mother of Jesus?
8. What can you do to improve your commitment to God and your relationships with others?
9. What is the new commandment given by Jesus to us? Why is it important for us to obey this commandment? (John 13:34–35).
10. Why is it so difficult for us to forgive others when they have wronged us? What are the consequences of an unforgiving heart?

# Notes

Chapter One

Behind Door One
The Woman of Samaria: Discovering the Living Water

1. Matthew Henry, Matthew Henry's Commentary on the Whole Bible: Complete and unabridged, (Peabody, Massachusetts: Hendrickson Publishers, 2008), pp. 894-895.
2. Ibid.
3. John MacArthur, Twelve Extraordinary Women, How God shaped women of the bible and what He wants to do with you, (Nashville: Thomas Nelson Publishers, 2005), p. 142.
4. In Adam Clarks Commentary on the Whole Bible (Ref. Josephus Ant. 1.xi.c.8).
5. Charles H. Spurgeon, C.H. Spurgeon's Sermons On Women of the New Testament, (Grand Rapids: Zondervan Publishing House, 1959), p. 56.
6. Gary M. Burge, Encounters with Jesus, (Grand Rapids: Zondervan, 2010), pp. 102-103.
7. Catherine Clark Kroeger, Mary J. Evans, The IVP Women's Bible Commentary, (Downers Grove, IL: Intervarsity Press, 2002), pp. 70-81.
8. Ibid., 597.

## Chapter Two

**Behind Door Two**
**Abigail: When Beauty Marries a Fool**

1. Matthew Henry, Matthew Henry's Commentary on the Whole Bible: Complete and unabridged, (Peabody, Massachusetts: Hendrickson Publishers, 2008), p. 337.
2. Herbert Lockyer, All the Women of the Bible, (Grand Rapids: Zondervan Publishing House, 1988), p. 23.
3. J.I. Packer, M.C. Tenney, Manners and Customs of the Bible, (Nashville: Thomas Nelson Publishers, 1980), p. 432.

## Chapter Three

**Behind Door Three**
**Mary Magdalene: From Demons to Devotion**

1. Herbert Lockyer, All the Women of the Bible, (Grand Rapids: Zondervan Publishing House, 1988), p. 100.
2. Ibid.
3. John MacArthur, Twelve Extraordinary Women, How God shaped women of the bible and what He wants to do with you, (Nashville: Thomas Nelson Publishers, 2005), p. 172.
4. Ibid., 173.
5. Ibid., 174.
6. Matthew Henry, Matthew Henry's Commentary on the Whole Bible: Complete and unabridged, (Peabody, Massachusetts: Hendrickson Publishers, 2008), p. 1332.
7. Herbert Lockyer, All the Women of the Bible, (Grand Rapids: Zondervan Publishing House, 1988), pp. 106-107.
8. Ibid., 150.
9. Matthew Henry, Matthew Henry's Commentary on the Whole Bible: Complete and unabridged, (Peabody,

Massachusetts: Hendrickson Publishers, 2008), pp. (1520-1521).
10. Catherine Clark Kroeger, Mary J. Evans, The IVP Women's Bible Commentary, (Downers Grove, IL: Intervarsity Press, 2002), p. 600.

Chapter 4

Behind Door Four
Tamar: A Defiled Princess in Isolation

1. J.D. Douglas, Merrill C. Tenney, Zondervan Illustrated Bible Dictionary, (Grand Rapids: Zondervan, 1987/2011) p. 899.
2. Herbert Lockyer, All the Women of the Bible, (Grand Rapids: Zondervan Publishing House, 1988), p. 86.
3. J.I. Packer, M.C. Tenney, Illustrated Manners and Customs of the Bible, (Nashville: Thomas Nelson Publishers), p. 320.
4. J.D. Douglas, Merrill C. Tenney, Zondervan Illustrated Bible Dictionary, (Grand Rapids: Zondervan, 1987/2011), p. 151.
5. Jeffrey C. Geoghegan, Israelites Sheepshearing and David's Rise to Power, In Biblical Studies on the Web, Vol. 87, (2006), pp. 55-63.
6. John MacArthur, The MacArthur Bible Commentary, (Nashville: Thomas Nelson, Inc., 2005), p. 369.

Chapter 5

Behind Door Five
Hannah: A Prayer and a Vow Fulfilled

1. J.I. Packer, M.C. Tenney, Illustrated Manners and Customs of the Bible, (Nashville: Thomas Nelson Publishers), p. 625.
2. Ibid., 625.

3. Matthew Henry, Matthew Henry's Commentary on the Whole Bible: Complete and unabridged, (Peabody, Massachusetts: Hendrickson Publishers, 2008), p. 303.
4. Ibid., 303.
5. Ibid.
6. John MacArthur, The MacArthur Bible Commentary, (Nashville: Thomas Nelson, Inc., 2005), p. 1643.

Chapter 6

Behind Door Six
Leah: Comforted by Her Children

1. William Whiston, Josephus, The Complete Works, (Nashville: Thomas Nelson Publishers, Inc., 1998), pp. 55-56.
2. Matthew Henry, Matthew Henry's Commentary on the Whole Bible: Complete and unabridged, (Peabody, Massachusetts: Hendrickson Publishers, 2008), p. 51.
3. H. V. Morton, Women of the Bible, (New York: Dodd, Mead & Company, 1942), p. 43.
4. J.D. Douglas, Merrill C. Tenney, Zondervan Illustrated Bible Dictionary, (Grand Rapids: Zondervan, 1987/2011), p. 1146.
5. John MacArthur, The MacArthur Bible Commentary, (Nashville: Thomas Nelson, Inc., 2005), p. 58.

Chapter 7

Behind Door Seven
Esther: A Queen for Such a Time as This

1. Herbert Lockyer, All the Women of the Bible, (Grand Rapids: Zondervan Publishing House, 1988), p. 165

## Notes

2. Ibid., 166.
3. Matthew Henry, Matthew Henry's Commentary on the Whole Bible: Complete and unabridged, (Peabody, Massachusetts: Hendrickson Publishers, 2008), p. 512.
4. Flavius Josephus, Josephus the Complete Works, Translated by William Whiston, (Nashville: Thomas Nelson Publishers, 1998), pp. 357-358.
5. Ibid., p. 358.
6. Herbert Lockyer, All the Women of the Bible, (Grand Rapids: Zondervan Publishing House, 1988), p. 52.
7. www.Israel-a-history-of.com/QueenEsther-of-the-Bible.html.
8. Ibid.
9. Archeological Study Bible, New International Version, (Grand Rapids: Zondervan Publishers, 1978), p. 120.
10. Matthew Henry, Matthew Henry's Commentary on the Whole Bible: Complete and unabridged, (Peabody, Massachusetts: Hendrickson Publishers, 2008), p. 513.
11. Ibid., p. 514.

Chapter 8

Behind Door Eight
Jezebel: The Wicked Shall Cease from Troubling

1. J.D. Douglas, Merrill C. Tenney, Zondervan Illustrated Bible Dictionary, (Grand Rapids: Zondervan, 1987/2011), pp. 1128-1129.
2. Lesley Hazelton, Jezebel: The Untold Story of the Bible's Harlot Queen. (New York: Doubleday, 2007), pp 25-26.
3. Herbert Lockyer, All the Women of the Bible, (Grand Rapids: Zondervan Publishing House, 1988), p. 74.

*Notes*

4. J.D. Douglas, Merrill C. Tenney, Zondervan Illustrated Bible Dictionary, (Grand Rapids: Zondervan, 1987/2011), p. 149.
5. Ibid., p. 130.
6. Matthew Henry, Matthew Henry's Commentary on the Whole Bible: Complete and unabridged, (Peabody, Massachusetts: Hendrickson Publishers, 2008), p. 416.

Chapter 9

Behind Door Nine
Naomi: Surviving the Storms of Widowhood

1. H. V. Morton, Women of the Bible. (New York: Dodd, Mead & Company, 1942), p.77.
2. Herbert Lockyer, All the Men of the Bible, (Grand Rapids: Zondervan Publishing House, 1958), p. 104.
3. Catherine Clark Kroeger, Mary J. Evans, The IVP Women's Bible Commentary, (Downers Grove, IL: Intervarsity Press, 2002), p. 149.
4. J.I. Packer, M.C. Tenney, Illustrated Manners and Customs of the Bible, (Nashville: Thomas Nelson Publishers), p. 335.
5. Catherine Clark Kroeger, Mary J. Evans, The IVP Women's Bible Commentary, (Downers Grove, IL: Intervarsity Press, 2002), p. 150.
6. Herbert Lockyer, All the Women of the Bible, (Grand Rapids: Zondervan Publishing House, 1988), p. 148.
7. Joan Chittister, The Friendship of Women: The hidden tradition of the bible, (New York: Blue Bridge, 2006), pp. 59-61.

*Notes*

Chapter 10

Behind Door Ten
Mary: The Sorrowful Mother at the Cross

1. Archeological Study Bible, New International Version, (Grand Rapids: Zondervan Publishers, 1978), p. 1623.
2. J.D. Douglas, Merrill C. Tenney, Zondervan Illustrated Bible Dictionary, (Grand Rapids: Zondervan, 1987/2011), p. 735.
3. Paul E. Miller, Love Walked Among Us: Learning to love like Jesus, (Colorado Springs, Colorado: NAVPRESS, 2001), p 35.
4. Matthew Henry, Matthew Henry's Commentary on the Whole Bible: Complete and unabridged, (Peabody, Massachusetts: Hendrickson Publishers, 2008), p. 1456.

Printed in Great Britain
by Amazon